Do Giraffes Sleep Standing Up?

... and more than 900 other trivia questions

Jon Wilman

BARNES
& NOBLE

NEW YORK

The author wishes to thank all those who provided questions, expertise, and encouragement: Rick Campbell, William MacKay, and Tommy Jenkins

Text design by Lundquist Design

2007 Barnes & Noble, Inc.

ISBN-13: 978-0-7607-8919-3
ISBN-10: 0-7607-8919-3

Printed and bound in the United States of America

10 9 8 7 6 5 4 3 2 1

Q **What animal is the world's tallest animal?**

A The male giraffe, which is the tallest of all land animals, can reach heights of just over 19 feet. The female giraffe is about two feet shorter than the male.

Q **What is the highest mountain in the world?**

A Mt. Everest, in Nepal and Tibet, is 29,028 feet above sea level. The five highest mountains in the world are all in the Himalayas.

Q **What is the highest point in North America?**

A At 20,320 feet, Mt. McKinley in Alaska is the highest mountain on the continent. The peak is also known by the Athabascan name Denali.

Q **What is the highest point in the 48 contiguous United States?**

A The summit of Mt. Whitney in California is 14,494 feet above sea level.

Q What is the lowest point on land in North America?

A Death Valley, also in California, bottoms out at 282 feet below sea level.

Q What is the lowest point on land in the world?

A Earth's lowest point on land is the shore of the Dead Sea in Israel and Jordan, which is 1,312 feet below sea level.

Q Hundreds of years before the arrival of Columbus, the Anasazi, or Ancient Ones, established their own thriving culture in the Four Corners region of America's Southwest. What was the most spectacular accomplishment of these ancestral Puebloans?

A The Anasazi's masterfully planned and executed cliff dwellings are among the architectural wonders of the New World. Each year, millions of Americans visit Mesa Verde National Park to see them.

For decades, archaeologists and historians have been debating the causes of the sudden collapse of the Anasazi empire in the late thirteenth century. Theories have ranged from rapid climatic changes to disease to warfare and even cannibalism.

Q According to a 2002 study released by Hagerty Classic Insurance (an American classic-car insurer based in Michigan), what is the single most dangerous food to consume while driving?

A Not surprisingly, hot coffee tops the top ten list of dangerous-while-driving foods. It is especially dangerous when consumed without a lid. Rounding out the list of top ten most perilous foods are: hot soup, tacos, chili-covered food, juicy hamburgers, barbecue, fried chicken, jelly doughnuts, soft drinks, and chocolate.

Q What states of the United States are the five most populous?

A According to a 2005 US Census Bureau estimate, California (36,132,000), Texas (22,860,000), New York (19,255,000), Florida (17,790,000), and Illinois (12,763,000) are the five states with the highest populations. Pennsylvania is a close sixth, with 12,430,000 people.

Q Which five states have the lowest populations?

A As of a 2005 US Census Bureau estimate, Wyoming (509,000 population) has the fewest people of the fifty states of the United States. Vermont (623,000), North Dakota (637,000), Alaska (664,000), and South Dakota (776,000) round out the bottom five in population of the fifty states.

Q **What did America's first Vice President, John Adams, say about the office?**

A John Adams, who didn't much care for the job, said " My country has in its wisdom contrived for me the most insignificant office that ever the invention of man contrived or his imagination conceived." John Adams later became the nation's second president.

Q **How many presidents were sons of presidents?**

A Two. In addition to the 43rd president, George W. Bush, who is the son of our 41st president, George H.W. Bush, John Quincy Adams, our sixth president, was the son of John Adams, our second president.

Q **Which famous American poet was invited to compose and read a new poem at John F. Kennedy's 1961 inauguration, but, because of the sun's glare, ended up reciting another poem from memory?**

A Robert Frost (1874-1963) recited "The Gift Outright" at the inauguration when the sun was in his eyes. He was unable to read the poem he had written for the occasion, "Dedication."

Q How many presidents have last names of only four letters?

A Five. Presidents George W. Bush, William H. Taft, George H. W. Bush, James K. Polk, and Gerald Ford.

Q Besides Lyndon B. Johnson, which American presidents were born in the great state of Texas?

A Only Dwight D. Eisenhower. Although they were Texas residents when elected, George Bush and his son, George W. Bush, were both New England-born.

Q How many presidents arrived at the White House with a PhD?

A Only one. Woodrow Wilson received his doctorate in political science from Johns Hopkins University in 1886, decades before he entered the Washington school of hard knocks.

Q What is the world's smallest fish?

A The smallest fish is the goby, which grows only as long as 1 centimeter (less than half an inch); it swims in coral reefs in the western Pacific.

Q What fish is the world's largest?

A The world's largest fish is the whale shark, which can grow to longer than 40 feet and can weigh as much as 30,000 pounds. Despite their huge size, they are not considered a threat to people. The whale shark is what's known as a filter feeder—it swims with its six-foot-wide mouth open, exposing its 600 tiny teeth, gathering small fish, crustaceans, and squid. The largest known whale shark was captured in 1919. It was over 60 feet long, and weighed 80,000 pounds! That's a lot of filter feeding!

Q What is largest freshwater fish found in the United States?

A The white sturgeon, which lives along the Pacific coast. One record-setting fish, reportedly weighing more than 1,500 pounds, was caught in Idaho's Snake River in the nineteenth century. The white sturgeon, which is typically ten to twelve feet in length, can live up to 100 years.

Q What fish is the fastest swimmer?

A The sailfish is considered the fastest of all fish species. It is difficult to measure the speeds of fish, but the sailfish has been clocked at speeds of over sixty miles per hour.

Q Some fish have cartilage for support, others have skeletons. What fish is the largest bony fish?

A The world's largest bony fish is the ocean sunfish, also known as the mola mola, which can grow to ten feet in length and weigh as much as 3000 pounds. There are larger fish, including sharks, but they have cartilage for support, rather than bones.

Q What is the largest living animal on land or in the sea?

A The blue whale, a mammal that is eighty to ninety feet long and has an average weight of 280,000 pounds! Its tongue alone weighs one ton! Not only is it the largest animal on earth, it is the loudest. Blue whales emit loud, low frequency rumbling sounds that register louder than a jet engine or a heavy metal rock band. They can emit sounds at a volume greater than 180 decibels.

Q Which animal is the largest land animal?

A The African elephant. The world's largest land animal can weigh more than eight tons and measure twelve to thirteen feet tall. The Indian elephant is a smaller elephant, but still can weigh as much as six tons.

Q What is the largest land animal in the United States?

A The American bison typically reach seven to eleven feet in length and weigh 900 to 2,200 pounds. Fully-grown bulls stand six feet or more at the shoulder. They can run nearly 30 miles an hour.

Q At the time of the arrival of the Europeans, what was the range of the American bison in North America?

A The American bison, commonly known as the buffalo, once roamed over all of North America, coast-to-coast, all the way from the West to the eastern seaboard. The size of the herd was estimated to be as high as 50 million animals. By 1900, there were fewer than 1500 bison left.

Q What are Gila monsters? Are they native to the United States?

A The Gila monster is a large, venomous lizard native to the deserts of Arizona and the American Southwest. It has a yellow and black tail, is eighteen inches long, with a stout body and a large head. Although it generally moves around slowly, it can bite suddenly and then hold on tenaciously to its victims.

Q What is the world's fastest land animal?

A It is believed to be the cheetah, which can attain speeds of 65-70 miles per hour in short bursts. Its acceleration is faster than the fastest cars.

Q Which animal is the fastest land animal in North America?

A The pronghorn. The Pronghorn can reach speeds around 60 miles per hour and can maintain a pace of 45 miles per hour for several minutes. The pronghorn's range extends from southern Saskatchewan and Alberta in Canada down to Sonora and Baja California in Mexico. The pronghorn is also known as the pronghorn antelope.

Q Where is the world's largest coral reef?

A The Great Barrier Reef, which is over 1,250 miles long, is off the coast of northeastern Australia.

The coral reef is largely formed from the buildup of many generations of algae and the limestone skeletons of tiny animals (corals) living in colonies. Coral reefs are found in warm shallow waters.

Q Who invented the gasoline-powered automobile?

A Germans Karl Benz and Gottlieb Daimler are both credited with developing the internal combustion engine automobile, because they were the first to make commercially viable autos. Daimler developed a 1.5 horsepower, two-cylinder gas-powered engine in 1886, and Benz, working separately, developed a gas-powered car at the same time.

Q When was the Ford Motor Company founded?

A In 1903, Henry Ford organized and became the president of the Ford Motor Company. Ford had built cars for several years prior to the founding of his company.

Q In what year was General Motors founded?

A The Olds Motor Company, the oldest unit of General Motors, was founded in 1899. General Motors was organized by William Durant in 1908, and included the Buick Motor Company, adding Olds in 1908 and Cadillac in 1909. By the 1920s, General Motors was the world's largest manufacturer.

Q Which car was the first to offer air conditioning?

A Packard exhibited an air-conditioned car at the Chicago Automobile Show in November 1939. But, the first fully automatic air conditioner was in the 1964 Cadillac.

Q When was the world's first car theft?

A It is believed to have taken place in June 1896, when a mechanic stole Baron de Zuylen's Peugeot.

Q Based on a 2006 study by Adrian White, a British social psychologist, which country was declared to be the happiest country in the world?

A Denmark. In his study, the main factors that affected happiness were health provisions, wealth, and education. White used data from 178 countries and more than one hundred studies; he admitted that collecting data on happiness and well-being is not an exact science.

Q Where do giraffes live in the wild?

A Only in central, eastern, and southern Africa.

Q What American-born man became Prime Minister and President of Ireland?

A Eamon de Valera, born in New York in 1882, became the Prime Minister, and later President, of the Republic of Ireland.

Q What American became Prime Minister of Israel?

A Golda Meir, born in Russia in 1898, grew up in Milwaukee after her family moved there in 1906. She was Prime Minister of Israel from 1969 to 1974.

Q How do snails manage to move across broken glass or even razor blades without injury?

A Snails secrete a special type of mucus that helps them move and protects them from injury.

Q In the sequence "2,3,5,7,11,13", what is the next number?

A 17. These are, in ascending order, the lowest prime numbers. Prime numbers are numbers that cannot be divided by any number other than itself and the number one.

Q What do Bob Dylan, Kevin McHale, and Greyhound Lines buses have in common?

A All three at one time called Hibbing, Minnesota home. Bob Dylan (Robert Zimmerman) was born in Duluth, but grew up in Hibbing, graduating from Hibbing High School in 1959. Kevin McHale, born in Hibbing in 1957, graduated from Hibbing High in 1976, the year he was named "Mr. Basketball" for the state of Minnesota. And, although it is now headquartered in Dallas, Texas, Greyhound was founded in Hibbing in 1914.

Q What is litmus paper? What do the colors indicate?

A Litmus paper is paper treated with a die that measures the acidity and alkalinity of a solution, or its pH. If the paper turns red, it is acidic; if it turns blue, it is alkaline.

Q What are the colors of the visible spectrum of light?

A Red, orange, yellow, green, blue, indigo, violet, which science students sometimes remember as "Roy G. Biv." Beyond the visible spectrum of light are ultraviolet, which is used in black lights and x-rays, and infrared, the most important use being remote controls for televisions.

Q What are quasars?

A Although scientific debates about the nature of quasars still rage, they appear to be stars that are moving away from earth at great speeds, as shown by the red shifts in their spectra. They may be distant galaxies.

Q Which actor successfully escaped *The Blob* (1958), but was unsuccessful in *The Great Escape* (1963)?

A Steve McQueen.

Q In *The Cincinnati Kid* (1965), the Kid takes on a stud-poker legend named Lancey Howard. Who played the aging card-shark?

A Edward G. Robinson. The Kid was played by Steve McQueen.

Q In *Breakfast at Tiffany's* (1961), Holly Golightly must repeatedly visit a man named Sally Tomato in prison and give him what?

A The weather report (which is, in reality, coded betting information). Holly Golightly was played by Audrey Hepburn.

Q Audrey Hepburn's first starring role was in a film directed by William Wyler. Name the movie, her occupation, her leading man, and the unusual thing that happened to the actress as a result of making the picture.

A Hepburn played a princess in *Roman Holiday* (1953), co-starring Gregory Peck. She won the Oscar for Best Actress in her first starring role.

Q The Quarrymen included the nucleus of what well known rock band?

A John Lennon, Paul McCartney, and George Harrison were all members of The Quarrymen. Ringo Starr joined much later, after they had become the Beatles.

Q What were the Who called before they were the Who?

A The High Numbers, who released one record in 1964, "I'm The Face."

Q What is the name of the only Broadway show tune recorded by the Beatles?

A "'Til There was You," from Meredith Wilson's *The Music Man.*

Q Which member of the Grateful Dead inspired an ice cream flavor?

A Cherry Garcia is a flavor of Ben and Jerry's ice cream (and frozen yogurt) named after the lead singer of the Grateful Dead, the late Jerry Garcia.

Q How high in the air can dolphins jump?

A Dolphins can jump as high as 20 feet in the air. They can be seen accomplishing this feat at various parks around the world, including Sea World in San Diego.

Q What was known as Seward's Folly?

A When the United States bought Alaska from Russia in 1867, the American press lambasted Secretary of State William Seward, who negotiated the deal, for the "outrageous" $7,200,000 purchase price.

Q In what year did Alaska become a state?

A Alaska became the 49th state of the United States in 1959. Hawaii also became a state in 1959.

Q How much do giant pandas eat every day?

A Giant pandas consume as much as 83 pounds of bamboo a day. They spend approximately 12 hours a day feeding. They are very picky eaters—although they will occasionally eat something other than bamboo, they prefer to eat only bamboo, and only fresh bamboo. They turn their noses up at frozen or freeze-dried product.

Q When was the Louisiana Purchase?

A In 1803, Napoleon sold 800,000 square miles of the Louisiana Territory to the United States for $11.25 million, plus U.S. assumption of $3.75 million claims from U.S. citizens. The total was $15 million. On March 10, 1804, a formal ceremony was conducted in St. Louis. The purchase doubled the size of the nation.

Q When did Lewis and Clark embark on their famous expedition to explore this new American land?

A On May 14th, 1804, Meriwether Lewis and William Clark left St. Louis to begin a transcontinental exploratory mission for President Thomas Jefferson. Their cross-country expedition took two and a half years.

Q When and where was Louis Armstrong born? When and where did Louis Armstrong die?

A Although he always claimed to have been born on the Fourth of July, 1900, recently uncovered records indicate that Louis Armstrong was born on August 4, 1901 in New Orleans. He died in his sleep of a heart attack in New York City on July 6, 1971.

Q The following musicians are best known by their nicknames. What were their birth names? Dizzy Gillespie? Duke Ellington? Count Basie? Cannonball Adderley? Fats Waller?

A John Gillespie, Edward Kennedy Ellington, William Basie, Julian Adderley, and Thomas Waller.

Q At a cost of over $30 million, *Heaven's Gate* (1980) has been credited with sinking a distinguished movie production and distribution company. Name the company, and also name the four early screen legends who started the original company.

A United Artists. Founded in 1919 by Mary Pickford, Douglas Fairbanks, Charlie Chaplin, and D. W. Griffith.

Q Name the only movie that actor Charles Laughton ever directed. It's an offbeat flick, based on a Davis Grubb novel.

A *The Night of the Hunter* (1955), starring Robert Mitchum.

Q Joel Cairo, Bridgit O'Shaughnessy, and a guy named Wilmer are all key players in what classic 1940s movie?

A *The Maltese Falcon* (1941), directed by first-time director John Huston. The above characters were played by Peter Lorre, Mary Astor, and Elisha Cook Jr.

Q How long was *The Garry Moore Show* on the air? What was the name of its announcer?

A *The Garry Moore Show* was on CBS from 1958 to 1964, and then returned in 1966 for a season. It starred Garry Moore, with Durward Kirby as the announcer.

Q What future TV comedy star got her start on Garry Moore's show?

A The show introduced Carol Burnett, who went on to have her own show (1967–1979) on CBS.

Q **Who was the moderator on *I've Got a Secret* from its debut in 1952 to 1964?**

A Garry Moore. Steve Allen hosted the show for a few years beginning in 1964.

Q **What popular musical variety show featured the Lennon Sisters? What were their first names?**

A Dianne, Janet, Kathy, and Peggy were the Lennon Sisters on the *Lawrence Welk Show.*

Q **How long was this musical variety show on the air?**

A Beginning in 1955, Lawrence Welk was on ABC for sixteen years, and syndicated for another eleven years. It's still on the air! The repeats of the old shows are being shown in syndication and on PBS.

Q **Who starred on the original television show *Dragnet* (1951–1959)? What character did he play?**

A Just the facts: Jack Webb played Sergeant Joe Friday.

Q Bo and Luke Duke were two of the most popular characters on television in the early '80s. Name the actors who played Bo and Luke. For extra credit, who sang the theme song and also served as the narrator on *The Dukes of Hazzard?*

A Bo was played by John Schneider and Luke was played by Tom Wopat on the series *The Dukes of Hazzard.* None other than country singer Waylon Jennings was the narrator and sang the theme song.

Q What is the literary significance of June 16, 1904?

A It's Bloomsday, the day in which all of the events of James Joyce's novel *Ulysses* occur.

Q Ernest Hemingway asserted that all modern American literature comes from one book. Which novel was Hemingway praising?

A Mark Twain's *The Adventures of Huckleberry Finn.*

Q "That's not writing; it's typing" was one American author's comment on another's work. Who was talking about whom?

A Truman Capote on Jack Kerouac.

Q **One famous American poet was a West Point cadet. Who was he and how did he fare?**

A Edgar Allan Poe's brief stint at the U.S. Military Academy brought mixed results. After less than eight months there, he was court-martialed and dismissed from the Academy in January 1831. However, before he left, Poe convinced more than 130 of his classmates to subsidize the publication of his second book of poetry.

Q **Which president of the Confederate States of America was a West Point graduate?**

A Jefferson Davis, the only President of the Confederacy, graduated from the United States Military Academy in 1828.

Q **At what location did the surrender by the Commanding General of the Confederate forces to the Commanding General of the Union forces take place?**

A On April 9, 1865, Confederate General Robert E. Lee surrendered to U.S. General Ulysses S. Grant at the Appomattox Courthouse, in Virginia. Both were West Point graduates.

Q How did Confederate General "Stonewall" Jackson earn his nickname?

A General Thomas Jonathan Jackson, also a West Point graduate, earned his nickname at the First Battle of Bull Run (1861), by holding his ground.

Q Which Civil war general popularized a new men's hairstyle, which became known as "sideburns"?

A Union General Ambrose E. Burnside earned a niche in history for his mutton chops, which became known as "sideburns." He, too, was a graduate of West Point.

Q Which future presidents graduated from West Point?

A Ulysses S. Grant, class of 1843, and Dwight David Eisenhower, class of 1915, both earned diplomas from the U.S. Military Academy.

Q Which future president graduated from Annapolis?

A Jimmy Carter graduated from the United States Naval Academy in 1946.

Q Name the first thirteen states of the United States.

A In the order of their statehood: Delaware, Pennsylvania, New Jersey, Georgia, Connecticut, Massachusetts, Maryland, South Carolina, New Hampshire, Virginia, New York, North Carolina, and Rhode Island.

Q Which eleven states seceded from the Union during the Civil War?

A South Carolina, Mississippi, Florida, Alabama, Georgia, Louisiana, Texas, Virginia, Arkansas, North Carolina, and Tennessee formed the Confederate States of America in 1861.

Q Six states do not have mansions for their governors to live in. Which six states do not supply the state's chief executive with a residence?

A Arizona, California, Idaho, Massachusetts, Rhode Island, and Vermont do not supply mansions for the Governor. They do supply cars for the Governors to get to work, though.

Q Twenty-three states of the United States are on seacoasts. Can you name them?

A Starting in the Northeast and going down the East Coast: Maine, New Hampshire, Massachusetts, Rhode Island, Connecticut, New York, New Jersey, Delaware, Maryland, Virginia, North Carolina, South Carolina, Georgia, and Florida. Continuing with Florida, and crossing the Gulf of Mexico: Alabama, Mississippi, Louisiana, and Texas.
On the Pacific: Alaska, Washington, Oregon, California, and Hawaii.

Q The capital city of a state is not always the largest city in the state. What are the capital cities of the following states: Kentucky? Wisconsin? Vermont? Pennsylvania? California? Washington?

A Frankfort, Kentucky; Madison, Wisconsin; Montpelier, Vermont; Harrisburg, Pennsylvania; Sacramento, California; and Olympia, Washington.

Q What is the largest lake in the world?

A The Caspian Sea, with a surface area of 143,244 square miles. This salty lake borders Azerbaijan, Russia, Kazakhstan, Turkmenistan, and Iran.

Q **Which states have the highest percentage of residents with college degrees?**

A According to US Census Bureau data from 2003, Massachusetts is the most-educated state, where 35.8% of the residents are graduates of a four-year college program. Massachusetts is followed by Colorado at 34.7%, Connecticut at 34.6%, Maryland at 34.5%, Virginia at 32.2%, New Jersey at 32.1%, Vermont at 32.0%, Minnesota at 30.6%, New Hampshire at 30.3%, and Washington at 30.2%. Although it is not a state, 44.2% of the residents of the District of Columbia have college degrees.

Q **By now, all good trivia readers know that George Washington never chopped down that famous cherry tree. Who told the lie?**

A To brighten his 1809 biography of the Father of Our Country, Parson Mason Weems concocted the edifying fable of George Washington and his hatcheted cherry tree.

Q **Which lake is the largest in North America?**

A Lake Superior is the largest lake in North America, the second-largest lake in the world, and the world's largest fresh water lake (by surface area). It has a surface area of 31,700 square miles and is approximately 350 miles long.

Q List the Great Lakes in order of size.

A From largest to smallest: Lakes Superior, Huron, Michigan, Erie, and Ontario.

Q Which Great Lake is the deepest?

A The deepest of the five Great Lakes is Lake Superior. Its lowest point is 1332 feet deep, almost enough to submerge the Sears Tower.

Q Which of the Great Lakes does not border on Canada?

A Lake Michigan is wholly in the United States, bordering on Illinois, Wisconsin, Michigan, and Indiana.

Q Where was the first women's right convention held?

A Organized by Elizabeth Cady Stanton, the first Women's Right Convention convened on July 19, 1848, in Seneca Falls, New York. A "Declaration of Sentiments and Resolutions" was issued at the convention. The Women's Rights National Historical Park and the National Women's Hall of Fame are both located in Seneca Falls.

Q Who was the first woman elected to the House of Representatives?

A Jeanette Rankin, Republican of Montana, was the first woman elected to the House of Representatives in 1916.

Q When did women get the right to vote in U.S. national elections?

A The ratification of the nineteenth amendment on August 18, 1920, guaranteed women access to the ballot box.

Q Who was the first woman sworn in as a Supreme Court Justice?

A Appointed by President Ronald Reagan, Sandra Day O'Connor took the oath in 1981.

Q Which nation was the first to give women the right to vote?

A New Zealand, in 1893.

Q When was soda first sold in a can?

A The first soda can was developed in 1938 by the Continental Can Company for Clicquot Club ginger ale of Mills, Massachusetts. RC Cola was the first soft drink company to nationally distribute soda in cans in 1954.

Q When did the Pillsbury Doughboy make his debut?

A The Pillsbury Doughboy made his first appearance in advertisements in 1965. His formal name is "Poppin' Fresh."

Q In 1592, Pope Clement VIII issued an edict allowing Christians to consume a particular beverage. He had been petitioned by priests to ban this beverage, but he refused. What beverage got his OK?

A Coffee, which is believed to be originally from Ethiopia, had been introduced to Europeans by Muslims.

Q The Galapagos Islands belong to what country?

A The Galapagos Islands are a province of Ecuador, located in the Pacific Ocean 500 miles west of the Ecuadorian coast.

Q How were Wheaties® invented?

A Wheaties® was discovered by accident in 1921, when a health clinician in Minneapolis, mixing a batch of bran gruel, spilled some on a hot stove. The gruel crackled into a crisp flake. Encouraged by the taste of the flake, he took the crisped gruel to the people at the Washburn Crosby Company, where the head miller, George Cormack, tested varieties of wheat before he developed the perfect flake. They introduced the cereal in 1924. In 1933, the advertising slogan "Wheaties—The Breakfast of Champions" was introduced.

Q Who was Charles Sherwood Stratton? How many people attended Charles Sherwood Stratton's wedding?

A The 3'4" tall Stratton was known to millions as Tom Thumb. When he married Lavinia Warren, a woman of short stature, on February 10, 1863, over 2,000 people attended the wedding at Grace Episcopal Church in New York City. They were married for twenty years, until his death in 1883.

Q What does R.S.V.P. mean?

A *Repondez, s'il vous plait.* Please respond.

Q What is the common name for iron oxide?

A Rust.

Q Did the U.S. Navy ever study Frisbees?

A Yes, they did—in 1968, the Navy spent almost $400,000 in a study of Frisbees in wind tunnels, using cameras and computers. We are not sure what they learned, but we are sure it was important.

Q What is the main component of most house dust?

A Dead skin cells. House dust is composed of human skin cells, animal and human dander, fibers from clothing and carpets, mold spores, food, plant residue, insect parts, pollens, and other minute solid particles. From the surface of our skin, 30,000 to 40,000 dead skin cells are lost per minute! But, these dead skin cells are replaced by the new skin cells growing underneath the surface.

Q Where is the world's first underground subway transit system?

A The London underground opened on January 10, 1863. Opened in 1897, Boston has the oldest subway in the United States. New York City's subway opened for business in 1904.

Q Where was the Lost Colony and how did it get lost?

A In 1587, English colonists reestablished a colony on Roanoke
Island, although the island had been the site of an Indian
massacre within the previous year. When Governor John
White returned from an extended trip to England in 1590, he
found the island deserted and plundered. Theories abound, but
no one knows for sure what had happened to the 117 settlers.

Q Where was tobacco first grown?

A The natives of the Americas used tobacco as long as 2,000
years ago. Columbus brought tobacco back to Spain, and its
use spread throughout Europe.

**Q On November 11, 1620, new colonists drew up and signed
one of the great documents in American history. What is the
name of this two hundred-word declaration and why is it so
important?**

A The Mayflower Compact. By signing the covenant, forty-one
Plymouth settlers agreed to establish a "civil body politic," a
government in their new home. Some historians regard the
compact as the beginning of constitutional government in
America. Others view it as a no more than a temporary
document designed to avert a mutiny.

Q How many legs does a spider have? How many eyes?

A All spiders have eight legs. Most spiders have eight eyes, but some have only six. There are spiders with two, four, and even twelve eyes.

Q How many arms does an octopus have? How many arms does a squid have?

A The octopus has eight arms. The squid has ten: eight arms and two specialized tentacles. The colossal squid is the largest creature on earth without a backbone, sometimes growing to 50 feet long and weighing about 1,000 pounds.

Q Why do spiders never get caught in their webs?

A Spiders can get caught in webs, but it rarely happens. The tips of their legs are specially built, and the oil in their legs keeps them free-footed.

Q How fast can dragonflies fly?

A They can achieve speeds of up to 30 miles per hour.

Q Why do fireflies flash?

A A chemical reaction related to the mating process causes the bursts of light. The male and female fireflies have different patterns of flashing, but it is much too complicated to discuss here.

Q Who was the first African-American to win the Nobel Peace Prize?

A Fourteen years before Martin Luther King Jr. won the honor, Ralph Bunche received the Nobel Peace Prize in 1950. Bunche earned the honor for his work as a mediator in Palestine while serving as the director of the United Nations Division of Trusteeship.

Q Who were the Tuskegee Airmen?

A The 332nd Fighter Group, known as the Tuskegee Airmen because they were the African-American graduates of the segregated pilot training program at Tuskegee, Alabama, set records for their aerial expertise in WWII.

Q What did Rosa Parks do on December 1, 1955?

A On December 1, 1955, she refused to give up her seat on a bus in Montgomery, Alabama. This act of bravery led to a boycott of Montgomery businesses, and was a major step in the battle for civil rights in the United States.

Q When did Jackie Robinson become the first black baseball player in the modern major leagues?

A Jackie Robinson, already a star in the Negro Leagues, joined the Brooklyn Dodgers in 1947.

Q Who was the first American president to be awarded the Nobel Peace Prize?

A The first U.S. president to win the Nobel Peace Prize is Teddy Roosevelt, who won the 1906 Nobel Peace Prize for drawing up the 1905 peace treaty between Russia and Japan. The other U.S. presidents who have been awarded the prize are Woodrow Wilson and Jimmy Carter.

Q Who invented the Spinning Jenny? What is it?

A In 1764, Englishman James Hargreaves invented a hand-powered machine, which, by adding spindles to the spinning wheel, was able to spin numerous threads simultaneously. This increased yarn production many times over. He named the machine for his daughter, Jenny.

Q What is the date of the first Wright Brothers airplane flight?

A On December 17, 1903, Orville Wright piloted the first heavier-than-air, machine-powered flight in the history of the world. Although it lasted only twelve seconds, his 120 feet flight over the sandy dunes of Kitty Hawk, North Carolina, made him and his brother Wilbur immortal. A later flight that day went 852 feet.

Q When was the zipper invented?

A Whitcomb Judson, an engineer from Chicago, patented the first zipper in 1893, and exhibited it at the Chicago World's Fair. However, the new invention didn't catch on (so to speak) until B. F. Goodrich put zippers in his new product—rubber galoshes. Goodrich also coined the term: Until then, zippers were called "hookless fasteners."

Q Match the inventors with the inventions.

Carrier	Machine gun
Babbage	Mercury thermometer
Nesmith	Air conditioning
Birdseye	Correction fluid
Gatling	Frozen food (commercial)
Fahrenheit	Calculating machine

A Carrier = Air conditioning; Babbage = Calculating machine; Nesmith = Correction fluid; Birdseye = Frozen food; Gatling = Machine gun; Fahrenheit = Mercury thermometer.

Q **We all know that Eli Whitney invented the cotton gin. But what is a cotton gin and why was the invention so important?**

A Whitney's 1794 "engine" (or "gin") enabled plantation owners to separate the sticky green seeds from short-staple cotton fiber in an efficient and cost-effective way. Thanks to Whitney's invention, the yield of raw cotton in the South doubled each decade after 1800.

Q **Under their birth names, Joe Yule Jr. and Frances Gumm, they never became stars. But under their stage names (and thanks to MGM) they became the biggest box office duo in musicals in the early 1940s. Name them.**

A Mickey Rooney and Judy Garland.

Q Make room for the moguls! Can you match the studio head with the studio he led:

    1. Adolph Zukor   a. Universal

    2. Darryl Zanuck   b. Columbia

    3. Harry Cohn   c. Paramount

    4. Carl Laemmle   d. Twentieth Century-Fox

A   1. Adolph Zukor – c. Paramount

    2. Darryl Zanuck – d. Twentieth Century-Fox

    3. Harry Cohn – b. Columbia

    4. Carl Laemmle – a. Universal

Q In this 1953 Western, Jack Palance plays a sinister hired gun named Wilson. He's "terminated" by the character whose name is the same as the movie's. Name the movie and the actor/terminator.

A *Shane*, starring Alan Ladd.

Q Why are oil, gas, and coal called fossil fuels?

A Because they are composed of the remains of organisms that lived long ago. Over the course of millions of years, these organisms decompose, and are converted into oil, gas, and coal.

Q Where is the largest oil field in the world?

A The largest oil field in the world is the Ghawar field in Saudi Arabia, which produces 4.5 to 5 million barrels of oil per day.

Q How many gallons are in a barrel of oil?

A The barrel, a standard measure of crude oil, contains 42 U.S. gallons.

Q Where was oil first discovered in the United States?

A The first oil well in the United States was in Titusville, Pennsylvania, where Colonel Edwin L. Drake drilled the world's first oil well in August 1859.

Q What does OPEC stand for?

A The Organization of Petroleum-Exporting Countries.

Q Are there any plums in plum pudding?

A Usually not. This English holiday dessert dating back to the Middle Ages contains suet, flour, sugar, raisins, nuts, and spices—but no plums.

Q What is a yak?

A A yak is a large, long-haired ox native to the high plateaus and mountains of Tibet, where the climate is cold and dry. The males are more than six feet high at the shoulder and weigh more than one ton. The wild yak, which is larger than the domesticated yak, is considered to be an endangered species.

Q Where are pandas found in the wild?

A In the wild, pandas are found only in three provinces of China: the Sichuan, Yunnan, and Shaanxi. Though their habitat once covered as much as 300,000 square miles, these migrating animals now live within an 83,000 square mile territory.

Q What is the largest living rodent?

A The capybara, a semi-aquatic rodent of South America, is about two feet tall at the shoulder, and can weigh more than a hundred pounds. Capybaras are shorthaired, brownish rodents, with blunt snouts, short legs, small ears, and almost no tail. South American capybaras can be up to four feet long; Panamanian capybaras are a little smaller. They are vegetarians, and like to eat in people's gardens.

Q What was the name of the Ewings' ranch on the TV show *Dallas* (1978-1991)?

A South Fork.

Q Which actors played the following TV doctors: Dr. Kildare? Ben Casey? Dr. Anderson on *Father Knows Best*? Dr. Ross on *E.R.*?

A They were played, respectively, by Richard Chamberlain, Vince Edwards, Robert Young, and George Clooney.

Q *The Honeymooners* (1952–1957) centered around Jackie Gleason's Ralph Kramden. What did Ralph do for a living? Where did Ed Norton, played by Art Carney, work?

A Ralph was a bus driver. Norton, Ralph's upstairs neighbor and good buddy, worked in the sewers.

Q Where did Ralph, Alice, Ed, and Trixie live?

A In an apartment building on Chauncey Street, in the Bensonhurst section of Brooklyn.

Q Warren Beatty appeared as a regular in what popular fifties sitcom?

A In the 1959–1960 season of *The Many Loves of Dobie Gillis*, Beatty played Milton Armitage, Dobie's rich rival for the affections of Thalia Menninger (played by Tuesday Weld).

Q Who was the narrator on the 1950s television series *The Untouchables?*

A Newspaperman and gossip columnist Walter Winchell received $25,000 to narrate each episode of this weekly drama. On this partially fact-based show, machine-gun wielding gang-buster Eliot Ness (portrayed by Robert Stack) tracked down assorted real-life mobsters, such as Frank Nitti (played by Bruce Gordon.) The show, which aired from 1959 to 1963, was among the most violent—and popular—shows of its time.

Q What was the name of the character played by Ted Danson on the television comedy *Cheers* (1982–1993)? What was the name of his girlfriend for the first five seasons, who was played by Shelly Long?

A Sam Malone, former pitcher for the Boston Red Sox. Diane Chambers was his on-again off-again girlfriend.

Q Where are the Weddell and Ross Seas?

A Antarctica

Q Who was the first person to reach the South Pole?

A The Norwegian explorer Roald Amundsen on December 13, 1911.

Q What percentage of the world's fresh water is in the frozen ice mass of Antarctica?

A 70 %.

Q What's the name of the movie star character Gene Kelly plays in the 1952 musical *Singin' in the Rain*? How about the name of his glamorous silent screen leading lady? What's the name of the studio where the character played by Gene Kelly works?

A Kelly plays Don Lockwood; actress Jean Hagen plays Lina Lamont. Monumental Pictures.

Q One of the most famous scenes in movie history is Gene Kelly's dancing through the rain while singing the title song of *Singin' in the Rain*. Name the types of stores Kelly passes while performing this number.

A A women's clothing store, a drugstore, a music studio, a millinery shop, a book store, and the Mount Hollywood Art School.

Q Who bites more frequently, male or female mosquitoes?

A Male mosquitoes do not bite humans. Instead, these little vegetarians live on plant sap and juices.

Q One team won eight consecutive National Basketball Association (NBA) Championships. What team? Which years?

A The Boston Celtics won NBA titles every year from 1959 through 1966.

Q How many seasons did the American Basketball Association (ABA) survive?

A Nine seasons; from 1967 to 1976. After the league ceased operations, four ABA teams joined the National Basketball Association: Indiana, Denver, San Antonio, and the New York Nets.

Q Who holds the record for most lifetime points in the NBA?

A During his career, Kareem Abdul Jabbar scored 38,387 points.

Q What team has won the most NCAA championships in men's basketball?

A UCLA has won eleven NCAA championships. The University of Kentucky is second, having won the crown seven times.

Q When did Alfred E. Neuman first appear in *MAD* magazine?

A Alfred appeared in Issue #29 (September 1956); a portrait of him by Norman Minjo graced the cover of *MAD* one issue later.

Q The fictional character, John Clayton, Lord Greystoke, is better known by what name?

A Tarzan. Edgar Rice Burroughs's character Tarzan first appeared in the 1912 novel *Tarzan of the Apes*. There were twenty-three more novels with the Tarzan character; in the first novel, the young Lord Greystoke had been marooned in Africa, where he was raised by apes.

Q **Dr. Richard Mudd, who died in 2002, spent seven decades trying to clear his grandfather's name. Who was Dr. Samuel Mudd, and for what crime was he convicted?**

A   Dr. Samuel Mudd was one of eight convicted of conspiracy in the assassination of President Abraham Lincoln. Mudd had set John Wilkes Booth's broken leg and allowed him to rest in his home for several hours. Dr. Richard Mudd said that his grandfather did not know Lincoln had been assassinated when he treated Booth. Richard Mudd's son, Thomas, is continuing the fight.

Q **What son of a president was present at two assassinations of presidents?**

A   Robert Todd Lincoln (1843-1926), the son of Abraham Lincoln, was not present the night of April 14, 1865 when his father was shot, but he was present at two other presidential assassinations. He was present when President Garfield was shot in a Washington, D.C. train station in 1881, and when President William McKinley was shot at the Pan-American Exposition in Buffalo, New York in 1901.

Q **Where is Abraham Lincoln buried?**

A   President Lincoln is buried at Oak Ridge Cemetery in Springfield, Illinois.

Q Was the fictional character of Sherlock Holmes based on a real person?

A Dr. Joseph Bell inspired the character of Sherlock Holmes. In 1877, when Arthur Conan Doyle was studying to be a doctor in Edinburgh, Bell was one of his professors. Dr. Bell had excellent deductive abilities when observing people.

Q Match the comic strips with their creators.

1. *Doonesbury*	a. Chester Gould
2. *Dick Tracy*	b. Gary Larson
3. *Peanuts*	c. Walt Kelly
4. *Pogo*	d. Charles Schultz
5. *Far Side*	e. Garry Trudeau

A 1. *Doonesbury* — e. Garry Trudeau;
2. *Dick Tracy* — a. Chester Gould;
3. *Peanuts* — d. Charles Schultz;
4. *Pogo* — c. Walt Kelly;
5. *Far Side* — b. Gary Larson.

Q When did Mrs. O'Leary's cow cause the Chicago fire?

A Much of Chicago was destroyed by fire on October 8–11, 1871, but to this day it is unclear how it started. Mrs. O'Leary's bovine became the fall guy (cow).

Q In what year was gold first discovered in California's Sutter's Mill?

A 1848. On January 24 of that year, James Marshall panned the first gold nuggets there. By 1849, 80,000 prospectors had arrived in the territory. Within a few years, more than 500,000 people had migrated to California.

Q When did the Great San Francisco Earthquake strike?

A On April 18, 1906, San Francisco suffered its worst seismic upheaval. This quake and the fires and aftershocks that followed left 503 dead and caused $350 million in damages.

Q Who were the songwriters for many of Jackie Wilson's early records, including his first hit in 1957, "Reet Petite"?

A Berry Gordy, Jr. and Tyron Carlo Davis. Gordy went on to found Motown Records.

Q What was the title of the first hit record by James Brown and the Famous Flames?

A "Please, Please, Please," originally released on Federal Records in 1956, was not only their first hit; it was their first record.

Q Before they became famous, singers James Brown, Dean Martin, and Jackie Wilson all participated in what sport?

A In their youth, all three were amateur boxers. Jackie Wilson was even a Golden Gloves Champion in Detroit. Dean Martin boxed under the name of Kid Crochet.

Q Where was the original recording studio for Motown Records?

A Hitsville USA was the name given to the studios at 2648 West Grand Boulevard in Detroit where many of the first Motown hits were recorded.

Q What was the name of Dean Martin's partner in a popular song and comedy act?

A Dean Martin and Jerry Lewis were a popular team in the 1950's, making many movie, television, and radio appearances together.

Q Which river is the longest in the world?

A The longest is the Nile in Africa, which flows 4,160 miles to the Mediterranean Sea. The next two rivers in length are the Amazon and the Chang Jiang (Yangtze) Rivers.

Q Which lake is the largest in Africa?

A Lake Victoria, one of the sources of the Nile, is the largest lake on the continent. Its 28,820 square miles make it the third-largest lake in the world.

Q What is the longest river in the United States?

A There are two possible answers: The Mississippi River, which flows 2,340 miles from Lake Itasca, Minnesota, to the Gulf of Mexico, is the longest river in the U.S.; or the Mississippi-Missouri-Red Rock River system, which runs 3,710 miles from Montana to the Gulf of Mexico.

Q List the oceans in order of size.

A From the largest to the smallest: The Pacific, Atlantic, Indian, and Arctic oceans.

Q What countries does the Nile pass through on its way to the Mediterranean Sea?

A The basin of the world's longest river includes Burundi, Rwanda, Tanzania, Kenya, Uganda, Congo, Sudan, Ethiopia, and Egypt.

Q The Mississippi River forms one of the borderlines of ten different states on its voyage from its source in Minnesota down to the Gulf of Mexico. Can you name the states?

A After splitting the twin cities of Minneapolis and St. Paul, the Mississippi forms parts of the borderline of the states of Minnesota, Wisconsin, Iowa, Illinois, Missouri, Kentucky, Tennessee, Arkansas, Mississippi, and Louisiana. It empties into the Gulf of Mexico

Q Presidents Bill Clinton, George H. W. Bush, Ronald Reagan, Gerald Ford, Harry S Truman, Herbert Hoover, and James Garfield share one thing in common. What is that attribute?

A Each of them wrote left-handed.

Q Which president could write Latin with one hand and Greek with the other?

A James Garfield.

Q Who invented the Bowie knife?

A It is believed that Rezin Bowie invented the Bowie knife. However, it was his brother Jim Bowie who popularized it.

Q How did Jesse James die?

A   On April 3, 1882, while he was straightening a picture on a wall, James was shot in the back of the head by Robert Ford. Thereafter, Ford was known as "the dirty coward who shot Mr. Howard;" Howard being Jesse James' last known alias.

Q Who fought at the OK Corral on October 26, 1881?

A   As every cowboy movie-goer knows, the Earp Brothers and Doc Holliday exchanged gunfire with the outlaw Clanton Gang and the McLaury brothers. For added firepower, Virgil Earp, the sheriff of Tombstone, Arizona, had deputized his brothers Wyatt and Morgan.

Q What was Annie Oakley's birth name?

A   Phoebe Anne Moses. Although she never lived further west than Ohio, Annie Oakley won well-deserved fame as an expert rifle & shotgun marksman in Buffalo Bill's Wild West Show.

Q When was the Panama Canal opened?
a) 1899   b) 1903   c) 1906   d) 1914

A   d) The Panama Canal opened officially on August 15,1914.

Q Who created the metric system?

A Now used in most countries of the world, the French Academy
of Sciences devised the metric system in the late 18th century
to replace the non-compatible measuring systems then in use.
The scientists' goal was to standardize the measurements and
to use the decimal system rather than fractions.

Q When was the first running of the Kentucky Derby?

A Organized by Colonel Meriwether Lewis Clark, the first
Kentucky Derby was run in Louisville on May 17, 1875.

**Q Who else was shot during the assassination of President
John F. Kennedy on November 22, 1963?**

A Texas Governor John Connallly was seriously wounded
while riding in the presidential procession in Dallas.

**Q What famous actor was Ronald Reagan's best man at his
wedding to Nancy Davis in 1952?**

A William Holden

Q When did Sears, Roebuck and Co. begin?

A   A year after starting in Minneapolis in 1886, the R.W. Sears
    Watch Company moved to Chicago where they hired a Mr.
    Roebuck as a watchmaker. In 1893, Sears, Roebuck & Co. was
    formed and began to issue the first of its famous catalogues.

Q Which country has the largest population?

A   China has the world's largest population: an estimated 1.3
    billion people.
    India has the second largest population with just over one
    billion people.

Q Which country has the smallest population?

A   The one-half square mile Vatican city-state, with 1,000
    residents.

Q In which country do people speak the language Esperanto?

A   Nowhere. It is an artificial international language, which
    never became accepted.

Q **What do Istanbul, Constantinople, and Byzantium have in common?**

A They are three historical names for the same city, present-day Istanbul.

Q **What historic event occurred on July 14, 1789?**

A On that day, an angry French crowd stormed Paris's Bastille Prison. July 14th is now commemorated in France as Bastille Day.

Q **What happened on June 28, 1914?**

A On June 28, 1914, a Serbian activist assassinated Archduke Francis Ferdinand, the heir to the throne of Austria-Hungary, and his wife, in Saravejo. Within two months, tensions had escalated into the First World War.

Q **When was the Berlin Wall built? When did it come down?**

A The Berlin Wall was constructed in August 1961 to stop escapes by East Germans to West Berlin. The wall was dismantled in 1989.

Q When did World War Two begin?

A The actual fighting began when German troops crossed the
border into Poland on September 1, 1939. Pledged to
support Poland, Britain and France declared war on
Germany two days later. The United States did not enter the
war until December 1941.

**Q What was the only country that Germany declared war on
in World War Two?**

A On December 11, 1941, Germany declared war on the
United States. Germany did not have official declarations of
war with the other countries with which it was at war.

Q How many people died in the Flu Epidemic of 1918–1919?

A In the three waves of the 1918–1919 Flu Epidemic, at least
twenty million people succumbed. Indeed, many estimates
run as high as thirty million dead. Coming on the heels of
the First World War (in which *only* ten million perished),
the pandemic spread more quickly and widely because of
the large troop movements of the time.

Q When was the first drive-in movie opened?

A Richard Hollingshead opened a drive-in movie theatre in Camden, New Jersey on June 6, 1933. He hoped it would be enough of an attraction to boost sales at his gas station. It was sold out the first night (the first film shown was *Wife Beware*), and for many nights after that.

Q In a 1988 movie, Sally Field and Tom Hanks were paired as potential lovers. Only a few years later, in 1994, Sally Field played Tom Hanks's mother. Name these two films.

A *Punchline* (1988) and *Forrest Gump* (1994).

Q Who was the actor who played Staff Sgt. Raymond Shaw in the original 1962 version of *The Manchurian Candidate*? What is the name of the actress who played his "cool as a cucumber" mother? What was the actual age difference between the actor playing Staff Sgt. Shaw and his screen mother in *The Manchurian Candidate*?

A Laurence Harvey. Angela Lansbury played his mother; Lansbury was three years older than Laurence Harvey.

Q Joey on *Friends* (1994-2004) got a big break in his career when he was cast on a soap opera. What soap was he on? Unfortunately, his character died in a tragic accident. How did he die?

A *Days of Our Lives*. After being insulted by Joey, the writers on *Days of Our Lives* had his character, Dr. Drake Ramore, fall down an elevator shaft.

Q Although *The Matrix* (1999) takes place in a fictional city, the street names can all be found in what American city?

A Chicago, which is the hometown of writers/directors Larry and Andy Wachowski.

Q Who played the character Liz Teel in the unrelated 1993 television series *The Matrix*?

A Carrie-Anne Moss, who also plays Trinity in the 1999 film *The Matrix*.

Q When did MTV make its debut?

A August 1, 1981. It kicked off at midnight with a video of the British band The Buggles: *Video Killed the Radio Star*.

Q When did *The Real World* show premiere on MTV?

A May 21, 1992. It was perhaps the first of a new breed of reality TV shows. Seven strangers were chosen to live together and have cameras record their lives.

Q What movie star invented a radio controlled torpedo?

A Hedy Lamarr, who was born in Austria as Hedwig Eva Kiesler, was both a movie star and an inventor. She starred in several MGM films, including *Algiers* (1938) and *White Cargo* (1942), but she also was granted a patent for a type of radio controlled torpedo. The technology she invented was later used in satellite technology.

Q Who is the inventor of the Veg-O-Matic food slicer, the Smokeless Ashtray, the Showtime Rotisserie, and the Inside-the-Shell Egg Scrambler? This marketing genius also invented the Mince-O-Matic and the Chop-O-Matic.

A As every late-night-TV-watcher knows, the inventor of all of these products and also GHL hair-in-a-can spray is Ron Popeil. But, wait, there's more! Ron, an avid fisherman, also invented the Popeil Pocket Fisherman (yours for only $19.99). Popeil sold his company, Ronco Products, for $55 million dollars in 2005.

His autobiographical 2001 book was modestly titled *The Greatest Salesman of the Century*.

Q Who invented the La-Z-Boy reclining chair?

A Edwin Shoemaker, working with his cousin Edward Knabush, came up with the idea in 1928. And, sitting down, or lying back, has never been the same. They started upholstering the chairs in 1929, and they came up with the La-Z-boy name the same year.

Q Who was the only heavyweight boxing champion to end his career undefeated?

A When he retired from boxing in 1956, heavyweight champion Rocky Marciano had a professional record of 49 victories and no defeats or draws. He had held the world championship for four years.

Q When did Joe Louis first become the heavyweight champion?

A On June 22, 1937, Joe Louis, also known as "The Brown Bomber," knocked out James J. Braddock, thus beginning a twelve-year reign as the world heavyweight champion.

Q What boxer was nicknamed the "Manassa Mauler"?

A Born in Manassa, Colorado, former barroom bouncer Jack Dempsey.

Q What fight was "The Thrilla in Manila"?

A The aptly named Muhammad Ali-Joe Frazier championship fight in 1975. Ali won the hard-fought match when Frazier was unable to come out for the 15th round.

Q Annette Funicello made her television debut on what afternoon show?

A Annette was a Mouseketeer on the original daily afternoon *Mickey Mouse Club* (1955–1959).

Q What former Mouseketeer played Jeff Stone on *The Donna Reed Show* (1958–1966)?

A Paul Peterson played the son of Donna Reed and Carl Betz on *The Donna Reed Show*, a classic family sitcom of the late 1950s. Shelley Fabares played his sister, Mary.

Q What future sitcom star had a short role on the 1980s series *Benson*?

A Jerry Seinfeld played Frankie on *Benson*, which starred Robert Guillaume as the title character.

Q **What was James Cagney's first film? What was the last film in which Cagney appeared?**

A James Cagney's first film was *Sinner's Holiday*, which was released in 1930; he had played the same part in the 1929 Broadway show. Cagney's last theatrical release in 1981 was *Ragtime*, in which he played Police Chief Rheinlander Waldo. He was also in a 1984 television movie titled *Terrible Joe Moran*, in which he teamed up with Art Carney. Cagney, born in 1899, died in 1986.

Q **What top-rated TV drama series, which debuted in 1981, starred an ex-wife of the President of the United States? The plot revolved around family disputes over the control of a vineyard.**

A *Falcon Crest* debuted on December 4, 1981, starring Robert Foxworth, Susan Sullivan, Lorenzo Lamas, and Jane Wyman, who was once married to Ronald Reagan, as the matriarch Angela Channing.

Q **What is the date of the Magna Carta?**

A King John of England signed the Magna Carta in 1215, which guaranteed the privileges of nobles and church against the monarchy, and also assured jury trial.

Q Who fought in the Hundred Years War? Did it really last a hundred years?

A France and England were officially at war from 1334 to 1453, but during much of that time they fought few battles. It was not until 1565 that the English were forced out of Calais, their last foothold on the French mainland.

Q When did Marco Polo go to China?

A In 1260, Marco Polo, son of a Venetian merchant and explorer, accompanied his father on an overland journey to China. His record of his Asian adventures, written while he was imprisoned, became the most famous travel book in history.

Q What are the names of the wives of Henry the Eighth?

A Henry VIII, who ruled England from 1509 to 1547, married six times. His not always-so-lucky wives were: Catherine of Aragon, whom he divorced; Anne Boleyn, whom he beheaded; Jane Seymour, who died during childbirth; Anne of Cleves, divorced; Catherine Howard, another decapitation; and Catherine Parr, who, somehow, outlived him.

Q In which city was the first electric traffic light installed?

A Cleveland, Ohio. When Garrett Morgan installed his device on the corner of East Euclid & East 105th Street, no other city in the world had an electric traffic signal. Morgan, the son of a freed slave, can be credited also with another life-saving invention: the gas mask.

Q How many of the Allman Brothers were actually brothers?

A Two: Duane and Gregg.

Q How were the Beach Boys related?

A Three of the original Beach Boys were brothers—Brian, Carl, and Dennis Wilson. One, Mike Love, was a cousin, and the other, Al Jardine, was a neighbor.

Q What was the relationship between Gladys Knight and the Pips?

A Gladys' back-up singers, the Pips, consist of two of her cousins, and her brother, Merald ("Bubba").

Q How were the BeeGees related?

A Robin, Barry, and Maurice Gibb were brothers.

Q What were the names of the identical cousins on *The Patty Duke Show* (1963–1966)?

A Patty Lane and Cathy Lane, both played by Patty Duke.

Q What are the names of the nephews of Donald Duck?

A Huey, Dewey, and Louie.

Q What is Scrooge McDuck's relationship to Donald Duck?

A Scrooge McDuck is Donald's billionaire uncle. He is believed to be the brother of Donald's mother.

Q When was the Star Spangled Banner written? What inspired Francis Scott Key to write "The Star-Spangled Banner"?

A Francis Scott Key wrote the American national anthem after watching the unsuccessful bombardment of Baltimore's Fort McHenry by British ships on the night of September 14, 1814.

Q When did the Erie Canal open?

A The first boat left Buffalo on October 26, 1825 and arrived in New York City on November 4. By connecting Lake Erie to the Hudson River, the Erie Canal radically decreased the shipping time between cities in the interior and the Atlantic coast.

Q What is the Monroe Doctrine?

A In 1823, President James Monroe declared that the Americas were to be free from colonialism and interference from Europe.

Q Remember the Alamo! What happened at the Alamo?

A Under siege by thousands of Mexican soldiers led by dictator Santa Ana, the 189 defenders of the Texas Republic at the Alamo held out for 13 days to the last man—from February 23 to March 6, 1836. Among the illustrious defenders were William Travis, Davy Crockett, and Jim Bowie.

Q Which bird is the fastest flyer?

A The peregrine falcon can reach speeds of up to 200 miles per hour when diving for such prey as doves and pigeons.

Q Which bird is the largest living bird?

A The largest extant bird is the ostrich. Male ostriches grow to about nine feet tall and weigh over 300 pounds. Ostriches may be flightless birds, but they are fast on their feet, capable of running at 45 miles per hour.

Q What bird is the world's smallest living bird?

A The bee hummingbird, native to Cuba, weighs less than one ounce and measures about two inches.

Q Where do secretary birds live? How do secretary birds subdue their prey?

A Secretary birds, three-foot-tall birds with long legs, live in Africa south of the Sahara. These birds of prey use their strong legs to kickbox, pounding the daylights out of reptiles, snakes, lizards, and small ground rodents. They are named secretary birds because the plume feathers at the back of their heads resemble old-fashioned quill pens.

Q Do birds have the sense of smell?

A Based on scientific studies of bird brains, the sense of smell seems to be underdeveloped in most birds. Not too surprisingly, a large part of the brain is connected to sight and balance—both very important when flying.

Q Do any mammals lay eggs?

A Yes, both the spiny anteater and the duck-billed platypus are mammals and lay eggs.

Q What kind of animal is a pinniped? What is the largest pinniped?

A A pinniped is an aquatic carnivorous mammal that has four flippers. The name "pinniped" refers to the animal being "fin-footed." Seals, sea lions, and walruses are all pinnipeds. The largest pinniped is the elephant seal, which can weigh as much as four tons.

Q What is a polar bear's favorite treat?

A Polar bears, the world's largest land predators, like to eat seals. But, polar bears will eat other living things, such as rodents, birds, and walruses.

Q What movie has won the most Academy Awards?

A Three films, *Ben Hur* (1959), *Titanic* (1997), and *Lord of the Rings: The Return of the King* (2003), have each won eleven Oscars.

Q For what movie did Humphrey Bogart win his only Best Actor Oscar?

A *The African Queen* (1951).

Q What two actors won Oscars for playing the same character in two different films?

A Marlon Brando won Best Actor for playing the aged Don Vito Corleone in *The Godfather* (1972). Robert DeNiro won Best Supporting Actor for his portrayal of the younger Vito Corleone in *The Godfather Part II* (1974).

Q Name the classic epic movie—an Academy Award winner for Best Picture—that has no female speaking roles.

A *Lawrence of Arabia* (1962).

Q Ingrid Bergman won her second Best Actress Oscar for what film that also marked her return to Hollywood?

A *Anastasia* (1956). She won her first Best Actress Oscar for her role in *Gaslight* (1944).

Q Which faces of famous Americans appear on the following denominations of U.S. Currency: $1, $2, $5, $10, $20, $50, $100, $500, $1,000, $5,000?
Which of these famous Americans were not U.S. presidents?

A George Washington ($1), Thomas Jefferson ($2), Abraham Lincoln ($5), Alexander Hamilton ($10), Andrew Jackson ($20), Ulysses S. Grant ($50), and Benjamin Franklin ($100). William McKinley appeared on the $500 bill, Grover Cleveland was on the $1,000 bill, and James Madison appeared on the $5,000 bill, but these bills are no longer in circulation. Alexander Hamilton and Benjamin Franklin were not presidents of the United States.

Q Where was the game of golf invented?

A Scotland is considered the birthplace of the sport, golf having flourished there since the fifteenth century. Even then, an exerting round was followed by a refreshing trip to the local tavern.

Q Who has won more Masters tournaments than any other golfer?

A Jack Nicklaus, with six Masters victories.

Q When did Tiger Woods win the Masters tournament for the first time?

A On April 13, 1997, Tiger Woods won his first Masters tournament at Augusta National Golf Course.

Q Who was the first president to take up golf?

A William Howard Taft, who, despite some religious protests, inspired an American golf boom with his enthusiastic play.

Q Which of the following is not a member of the Professional Bowlers Association Hall of Fame?
Dave Ferraro   **Carmen Salvino**
Don Carter   **Roy Buckley**

A They all are.

Q Who was the first elected President of Russia?

A Boris Yeltsin, who was elected in June 1991. He was president from 1991 to 1999.

Q What was the name of the dynasty that ruled Russia from 1613 to 1917?

A The Romanovs. Descended from Michael Romanov, this dynasty included Peter the Great, Catherine the Great, and two Alexanders. Czar Nicholas II, the last Romanov ruler, was forced to abdicate in 1917.

Q Who was Rasputin?

A Grigori Rasputin was a Siberian peasant farmer and faith healer who wielded great influence with the Imperial Russian ruling family. Alexis, the son and heir to the Russian throne, suffered from hemophilia, the bleeding disease, and the Tsarina believed that Rasputin could heal him.

Q How did Rasputin die?

A On the night of December 16–17, 1916, three political opponents endeavored to kill Rasputin. First, they poisoned him, but it had no effect. Then, they shot him repeatedly, but, despite a torrent of bullets, Rasputin was still standing. Then the would-be assassins threw the notorious Mad Monk into the Neva River, where eventually he drowned.

Q What is the highest waterfall in the world?

A Angel Falls, on the Carrao in Venezuela, at 3,212 feet.

Q What is the highest waterfall in North America?

A Yosemite Falls, in California, with a total drop of 2,425 feet. The falls are actually in three sections: an upper waterfall's drop is 1,430 feet, with a lower one at 320 feet, separated by small plunges and rapids of 675 feet.

Q How high is Niagara Falls?

A Canada's Horseshoe Falls are 158 feet high, and 2,600 feet wide; the American Falls are 167 feet high, and 1,000 feet wide.

Q Where is the world's largest desert?

A The Sahara, in North Africa, encompasses 3,5000,000 square miles.

Q Where is the world's tallest active geyser?

A Steamboat Geyser, a popular attraction in Yellowstone Park, is the world's tallest active geyser. At irregular intervals, it sends water soaring as high as 300-400 feet. Less dramatic minor eruptions of 10 to 40 feet are much more common; Steamboat's major eruptions occur anywhere from four days to 50 years apart. About half of the world's one thousand active geysers are in Yellowstone Park.

Q Peter Lorre gets them and hides them in Humphrey Bogart's place of business. Bogart spends the film denying he has them, but finally gives them away. In the end, everybody's more or less happy. What articles am I referring to? In what movie?

A The letters of transit in *Casablanca* (1942).

Q Peter Lorre goes to Humphrey Bogart's place of business in order to find it. Bogart denies having it, but finally gives it to the people who want it. In the end, everybody's more or less unhappy. What article am I referring to? In what movie?

A "The stuff dreams are made of"...The leaden, fake Maltese Falcon in the movie of the same name.

Q What is the difference between a mammoth and a mastodon?

A Both are prehistoric proboscideans, but mammoths lived in grasslands, were ten to fourteen feet tall, and could weigh up to 20,000 pounds. Mastodons lived in forests, were only six to ten feet tall, and weighed only 8–10,000 pounds. Mastodons had flat heads and short tusks; mammoths had rounded heads and long tusks. Frozen, preserved mammoths have been found, organs intact, in the Siberian permafrost. Both species were herbivores.

Q Dolphins call to each other, but do dolphins have vocal cords?

A Dolphins, who are aquatic mammals, do not have vocal cords, nor do they speak with their mouths. They are able to make noises using their breath through the blowholes on the tops of their bodies.

Q What is the most prominent feature that the group of mammals known as proboscideans has in common?

A A proboscidean is a mammal with a long trunk-like snout. There are only two extant proboscideans—the African *(Loxodonta africana)* and Asian *(Elephas maximus)* elephants. Elephants are also called *pachyderms*, a term that refers to their thick skin.

Q Did the United States Navy use trained dolphins in Vietnam?

A Yes, dolphins were trained to conduct surveillance patrols with a camera held in their mouths, and work with frogmen to deliver equipment and to locate underwater mines and obstacles. The Navy denies rumors that the dolphins have been used to attack enemy ships and swimmers.

Q What is unusual about pregnant seahorses?

A Pregnant seahorses are male. The female seahorse transfers her eggs into the male's exterior abdominal pouch. The male grows visibly "pregnant" within a few weeks. Embryos hatch in his pouch and are incubated there.

Q What is a marsupial?

A A marsupial is a mammal with a pouch on the abdomen of the female, such as kangaroos, bandicoots, wombats, koalas, and opossums.

Q Where was the first skyscraper built?

A The building considered to be the world's first skyscraper is William Le Baron Jenney's ten-story Home Insurance Company Building in Chicago. Built in 1883, it was the first fully steel-framed building, using steel-girder construction, and supported by internal construction, rather than by load-bearing walls.

Q The Ryman Auditorium is well known as the home of what musical event? Where is it?

A The Grand Ole Opry, which has been a radio program for 75 years, moved to the Ryman Auditorium in 1943, and stayed there until the new Opry House was built in Opryland in 1974. The Ryman Auditorium is on 5th Avenue North in Nashville, Tennessee.

Q "More stars than there are in the heavens" was a 1940s slogan of which Hollywood studio?

A MGM

Q Where was William Shakespeare born?

A In Stratford-upon-Avon, England in 1564. He died on April 23, 1616, exactly fifty-two years after his birth.

Q In what year was the Globe Theater built?

A In 1599, the Globe Theater was constructed, utilizing timbers from another theater.

Q When was Christopher Marlowe born? How did he die?

A Marlowe was also born in 1564. He was killed in a tavern brawl on May 30, 1593.

Q   Which Elizabethan dramatist narrowly escaped the gallows for murder?

A   In 1598, Ben Jonson was almost executed for killing a fellow actor in a duel. Although he was reprieved, he was branded on the thumb for the felony.

Q   What is the name of William Shakespeare's wife?

A   Anne Hathaway. In 1582, Shakespeare married this farmer's daughter. She was twenty-six; he was eighteen.

Q   What did Shakespeare famously bequeath to his wife?

A   The only item Shakespeare specifically willed to his spouse was his "second best bed." Because the best bed in Elizabethan times was traditionally reserved for visitors, Shakespeare's bequest might have been a sign of endearment, rather than the slight it first seems. In any case, by law, Anne Hathaway received one third of her husband's estate.

Q Who fought in the Trojan Wars?

A A coalition of Greek principalities fought against Troy. This war was the subject of Homer's *Iliad*. It is believed that the wars took place in the 12th century B.C.E.

Q What was the Trojan Horse?

A According to classical literature, Odysseus conceived the clever idea of smuggling Achaean troops concealed in a wooden horse into Troy to defeat the hostile Trojans. Contrary to popular opinion, the horse was not presented to the unsuspecting Trojans as a gift: It was simply left in the abandoned Archaean camp outside the city walls. The Trojans took the bait, and the city was conquered.

Q Who were the combatants in the Persian Wars?

A The Greeks fought against the Persians for more than forty years, from 521 B.C.E. to 479 B.C.E. Herodotus' *History* provides much of the surviving information on this war.

Q Which ancient city-states were the main adversaries in the Peloponnesian Wars?

A Sparta and Athens. The First Peloponnesian War lasted from 431 to 421 B.C.E.; the second ended in 404 B.C.E. with Athens surrendering to Sparta. After this defeat, Athens went into a decline.

Q Match the U.S. cities and their nicknames:

Detroit	The Windy City
New York	Big D
New Orleans	The Motor City
Chicago	The Big Easy
Dallas	The Big Apple

A Detroit = The Motor City
New York = The Big Apple
New Orleans = The Big Easy
Chicago = The Windy City
Dallas = Big D.

Q Name the presidents portrayed on Mount Rushmore.

A From left to right: George Washington, Thomas Jefferson, Theodore Roosevelt, Abraham Lincoln.

Q What was the first capital of the United States?

A Both New York City and Philadelphia have a claim to the honor. George Washington was inaugurated as the first President at New York's Federal Hall and the first sessions of Congress under the Constitution were convened in that city. However, Philadelphia was considered the de facto capital at the time of the Declaration of Independence.

Q What does the state name "Oklahoma" mean in the Choctaw language?

A The name "Oklahoma" comes from the Choctaw words: "okla" meaning people and "humma" meaning red, so the state's name literally means "red people."

Q Which city is further east—Key West, Florida, or Lima Peru?

A Lima, Peru is four degrees east of Key West. In fact, most of South America is east of North America. Lima Peru at 77W longitude is east of Key West at 81W longitude.

Q Which location is further west—Washington Island, Wisconsin, or Pensacola, Florida?

A Pensacola. According to Jerry Rupiper of Washington Island Realty in Wisconsin, his office is at 86° 55'W longitude, which is further east than Pensacola Florida at 87° 13' W longitude

Q Who was the title character of the 1963–1966 television series *My Favorite Martian*?

A Ray Walston played the Martian who, disguised as Uncle Martin, lives with Timothy O'Hara (Bill Bixby).

Q When was the first episode of *I Love Lucy* shown?

A On October 15, 1951, CBS broadcast the first Lucy show. The episode was entitled "The Girls Want to Go to a Nightclub." The original show ran from 1951 to 1957.

Q What was the name of the club Ricky Ricardo owned on *I Love Lucy* (1951–1957)?

A Ricky Ricardo's Babalu Club. He originally worked at the Tropicana.

Q The family on the 1970s sitcom *The Brady Bunch* was too good to be true. What did Mike Brady do for a living to support his ideal family?

A Mike Brady, played by Robert Reed, was an architect.

Q The Brady boys were lucky enough to get visits from several famous athletes. What famous pitcher made a guest appearance? What NFL quarterback gave Bobby Brady a few pointers?

A Pitcher Don Drysdale. Joe Namath was the NFL quarterback.

Q Years before he appeared as a guest on *The Brady Bunch*, that same pitcher made a guest appearance on another TV sit-com—which one?

A *Leave It to Beaver* (1957-1963), where Don Drysdale took a long distance call from Beaver and Gilbert.

Q How do frogs tell us that the air pressure is decreasing?

A Frogs croak more often when air pressure drops. Low air pressure brings stormy weather.

Q Who invented the graham cracker?

A Rev. Sylvester Graham, a Presbyterian minister, developed the graham cracker in 1829 as a health food. Made from whole wheat flour, it was more of a digestive biscuit than a cracker. Graham was concerned that young Americans were too concerned with carnal desires, and he thought that a healthy vegetarian diet would help them control themselves. Today, most graham crackers are made from bleached white flour (which the good reverend opposed). And, they didn't stop carnal desires, anyway.

Q Do ducks sleep with their eyes closed?

A Yes and no. Ducks in the center of a group sleep with their eyes shut, but quackers on the edges will spend the night with one eye open.

Q How much gas do cows belch? (Why are cows seldom invited to parties?)

A Every day, the average cow emits thirty-five cubic feet of methane gas. Conferences on global warming have seriously discussed this embarrassing problem.

Q How far does a skunk spray?

A Skunks can spray their foul-smelling liquid up to 10 feet. However, this pungent aroma can drift downwind as far as a mile and a half.

Q When was *Scrabble*® invented?

A Unemployed architect Alfred M. Butt invented the game in 1931, but he couldn't settle on a name. He called his diversion "Lexiko," "It," and "Criss Cross," but made few sales. But, he and his partner James Brunot didn't mass produce games to be sold until 1948.

Q What is the best selling board game on earth and who invented it?

A Charles B. Darrow of Germantown, Pennsylvania, is generally credited with having invented the game of *Monopoly* in 1933. He patented *Monopoly* in 1935. More than 500 million people have played the game.

Q   How old is chess?

A   The prehistory and early history of chess are matters of great dispute. However, Chaturanga, which developed in India in the sixth century, has a strong claim to be the earliest clear ancestor of chess. The game entered Europe around the tenth century.

Q   What famous Egyptian city was founded by Alexander the Great in 331 B.C.E.?

A   After Alexander the Great conquered Egypt, he established Alexandria, naming the port city in his own honor.

Q   Who were the Vandals?

A   They were a Germanic tribe that conquered Spain and Gaul and sacked Rome in the 5th century.

Q   In what country are the remains of Petra?

A   Petra, which was founded by Nabataean Arabs, is located in present-day Jordan. Once an important trading center, the abandoned city was forgotten by the Western world for hundreds of years before being rediscovered in the early nineteenth century.

Q Who were the original Young Turks?

A The Young Turks were a coalition of Turkish nationalists and other reformers who, in 1908, seized power and forced the Sultan to restore a constitution and introduce social reforms, secularization, and industrialization in the Ottoman Empire.

Q Only three presidential candidates won at least 520 electoral votes in their race for the White House. Who are they?

A Franklin Delano Roosevelt garnered 523 in 1936; Richard Nixon, 520 in 1972; and Ronald Reagan, 525 in 1984. Each of them was running for a second term.

Q Name the four Chief Executives who won the White House after earlier being defeated as presidential candidates.

A Thomas Jefferson, Andrew Jackson, William Henry Harrison, and Richard Nixon. Sixteen years before Franklin Delano Roosevelt became president in 1936, he had been defeated as a vice presidential candidate.

Q All except one of the following presidents was defeated when he was seeking re-election. Name that president.

John Adams   Grover Cleveland

William McKinley   Herbert Hoover

Gerald Ford   William Howard Taft

George H.W. Bush   Benjamin Harrison

Martin Van Buren   Jimmy Carter

John Quincy Adams

A William McKinley was elected in both 1896 and 1900. Unfortunately, he was assassinated in 1901.

Q What Oscar-winning actor made a guest appearance playing Michael J. Fox's uncle on *Family Ties*?

A Tom Hanks.

Q What real-life couple met and fell in love on the television show *Bridget Loves Bernie*?

A Meredith Baxter became Meredith Baxter Birney after she fell in love with actor David Birney while they were playing Bridget and Bernie Steinberg on this 1972–1973 sit-com. The marriage lasted longer than the show, but, like the show, the marriage didn't last forever.

Q What was the single biggest problem that Steven and Elyse Keaton (played by Michael Gross and Meredith Baxter) on *Family Ties* had with their teenage son Alex?

A Alex (Michael J. Fox) was a conservative Republican. Elyse and Steven, his parents, were liberals. *Family Ties* aired from 1982 to 1989.

Q In what year did *The Beverly Hillbillies* first rumble into Hollywood, California?

A *The Beverly Hillbillies*, which starred Buddy Ebsen as the nouveau riche oil tycoon Jed Clampett, was first broadcast in 1962.

Q On the long running series *Bonanza* (1959–1973) there were three Cartwright boys. Name the actors and the characters. What was the name of the Cartwright's ranch?

A Pernell Roberts played Adam, Dan Blocker played Hoss, and Michael Landon played Little Joe. The ranch was The Ponderosa.

Q Alice was an aspiring singer, but had a day job as a waitress. Where did she work?

A Mel's Diner. The series *Alice*, starring Linda Lavin, ran from 1976–1985.

Q One of the biggest questions of the early 1980s was "Who Shot J. R.?" So, who did shoot J. R.?

A *Dallas*'s scheming J.R Ewing, played by Larry Hagman, was shot by his sister-in-law Kristin, played by Mary Crosby. Apparently Kristin was driven to a murderous rage when J.R. refused to marry her, like he had promised.

Q Who played Commander Adama on the late 1970s sci-fi series *Battlestar Galactica*?

A Lorne Greene, who also starred as the father of the Cartwright boys on *Bonanza*.

Q Which president gave the shortest inauguration address?

A George Washington's second inaugural speech lasted only two minutes. It consisted of a mere 133 words.

Q Who sewed the first American flag?

A Betsy Ross. Some rude debunkers have claimed that the Ross flag story was made out of whole cloth, but most historians and vexillogists (flag experts) agree that the widowed seamstress did indeed create the first American flag.

Q How many pounds of jellybeans were ordered by the White House during the Reagan administration?

A To satisfy Ronald Reagan's well known passion, twenty-four thousand pounds of jellybeans were ordered—and presumably consumed—by the staff of the White House during his two terms.

Q For whom was the stuffed toy, the teddy bear, named?

A It was named for President Theodore "Teddy" Roosevelt. While on a hunting trip in 1902, Teddy insisted that the hunting party put a wounded bear out of its misery. Eventually, with the help of cartoonist Clifford Berryman, the story changed to Teddy "rescuing" a wounded bear cub. Shortly thereafter, enterprising toy manufacturers named their toy bears teddy bears.

Q Eight presidents were born in one state. Can you identify the state and the presidents?

A Virginia. The eight presidents born within its borders were Washington, Jefferson, Madison, Monroe, William Henry Harrison, Tyler, Taylor, and Wilson. The runner-up state is Ohio, with seven presidential births: Grant, Hayes, Garfield, Benjamin Harrison, McKinley, Taft, and Harding.

Q What comment did Harry S Truman make concerning friendship in Washington, D.C.?

A As quoted by Helen Thomas, UPI White House correspondent, Truman said, "If you want a friend in Washington, get a dog."

Q What is the highest mountain in South America?

A Mount Aconcagua in the Argentine Andes is 22,834 feet above sea level.

Q Which mountain is the highest point on the continent of Africa?

A Kilimanjaro in Tanzania ranks as the highest mountain in Africa. Hemingway's favorite climb is 19,340 feet up.

Q What point is the highest in Australia?

A At 7,310 feet, puny by most standards, Mt. Kosciusko is nevertheless the highest mountain on the continent Down Under.

Q   Which of the fifty United States has the lowest high point?

A   Florida. No point in the Sunshine State is higher than Britton Hill, which is a mere 345 feet above sea level.

Q   On what day did Washington cross the Delaware?

A   On Christmas Day, 1776, General George Washington crossed the Delaware River. The following day, he surprised and defeated the Hessians at Trenton, New Jersey. The Patriots' pursuit of the German mercenaries might have been slowed by their discovery of a large cache of Hessian rum.

Q   Which American military leaders captured Fort Ticonderoga?

A   Americans Ethan Allen and Benedict Arnold surprised the British and captured Fort Ticonderoga on May 10, 1775.

Q   Besides Paul Revere, who else warned the good people of Concord that the British were coming?

A   Henry Wadsworth Longfellow's poem made Paul Revere immortal, but William Dawes and Samuel Prescott also braved that midnight ride on April 18, 1775.

Q **Where was Frank Sinatra born? What was the name of Sinatra's first group?**

A Francis Albert Sinatra was born in Hoboken, New Jersey on December 12, 1915. Sinatra sang as one of the Hoboken Four, who won a contest on *Major Bowes' Amateur Hour* in 1935. Frank was the lead singer.

Q **What role won Sinatra his Oscar?**

A Sinatra picked up the 1953 Best Supporting Actor award for his portrayal of Maggio in *From Here to Eternity*.

Q **"This wallpaper is killing me" are said to have been the last words of which famous author?**

A This was the last quip of the seemingly unflappable Oscar Wilde.

Q **When *Leaves of Grass* was first published in 1855, whose name appeared on the title page?**

A No one's. Walt Whitman's book might be the most important book in the history of American poetry, but its first edition was issued anonymously.

Q "April is the cruelest month" is the beginning of what major 1922 poem?

A T. S. Eliot opened *The Wasteland* with those now famous words.

Q Early in his career, Samuel Clemens took the nom de plume "Mark Twain." What does "mark twain" mean?

A "Mark twain" is a riverboat term meaning two fathoms deep (which is twelve feet). Former steamboat pilot Clemens took the name, he said, because "it has a richness about it; it was always a pleasant sound for a pilot to hear on a dark night; it meant safe water."

Q Where was Custer's Last Stand? Who were his opponents?

A General George Armstrong Custer and the Seventh Cavalry Regiment died in an 1876 battle at Little Bighorn River in southeastern Montana. At the time of the battle, Montana was still a territory.

The Sioux and Cheyenne warriors who fought Custer were led by Sitting Bull.

Q   In *A Clockwork Orange* (1971), Malcolm McDowell's character was particularly fond of what composer?

A   Beethoven, or as the character called him, "Old Ludwig Van."

Q   What is the name of the beleaguered country in the 1933 film *Duck Soup*? Name its President.

A   Freedonia is led by Rufus T. Firefly.

Q   What was the last movie in which Tracy and Hepburn appeared together? And the first?

A   *Guess Who's Coming To Dinner?* (1967). *Woman of the Year* (1942).

Q   What movie featured the first pairing of Bogart and Bacall?

A   *To Have and Have Not* (1944). It was Bacall's first film and Bogart's fiftieth.

Q Paul Newman and Joanne Woodward appeared together for the first few times in which two 1958 movies? In what movie did Newman direct Woodward?

A *The Long Hot Summer* and *Rally 'Round the Flag, Boys!* were their first two joint projects. Newman directed Woodward in *Rachel, Rachel* (1968).

Q "Fasten your seatbelts, it's going to be a bumpy night" is one of the most famous lines in movie history. In what film was it said? What actress (and character) delivered the line?

A Bette Davis (as Margo Channing) in *All About Eve* (1950).

Q When the lion roars at the beginning of an M-G-M movie, he's half-encircled by a Latin phrase. What is that phrase, and what does it mean?

A *"Ars Gratia Artis,"* which means "Art for Art's Sake."

Q What do birds dream about?

A According to a 1998 University of Chicago study, birds dream about singing. In fact, while asleep, zebra finches rehearse songs. When they awake, they warble more perfectly.

Q What is unique about the migration pattern of the Arctic tern?

A The Arctic tern breeds in the southern sections of the Arctic, and winters along pack ice near Antarctica—11,000 miles away! The distance that it travels is greater than that of any other species of bird.

Q What is unique about the migration of the Monarch butterfly?

A The Monarch butterfly migrates over 2,000 miles from its summer home in the northern U.S. and southern Canada to the mountains of central Mexico. The most fascinating part of this story is that the migrating butterflies have never before been to the southern winter grounds! The generation flying to the southern winter grounds was hatched in the summer grounds up north.

Q Is the tomato a vegetable or a fruit?

A Although many people think of the tomato as a vegetable, it is actually a fruit, because it is a seed-bearing ovary of a plant.

Q How did the laser get its name?

A Laser is an acronym for "light amplification by stimulated emission of radiation."

Q What symbol appears on the Canadian flag?

A A red maple leaf, with eleven points. Canada adopted a new flag
on February 15, 1965, doing away with the old Union Jack flag.

Q Match the Canadian provinces and their capital cities:

New Brunswick   Regina
Nova Scotia   Victoria
British Columbia   Halifax
Alberta   Fredericton
Saskatchewan   Edmonton

A New Brunswick=Fredericton
Nova Scotia=Halifax
British Columbia= Victoria
Alberta =Edmonton
Saskatchewan=Regina.

Q Which NFL team won the infamous "Heidi Bowl"?

A In November 1968, the Oakland Raiders beat the New York
Jets, 43–32, by scoring two touchdowns in the last 75 seconds
of the game. But television fans missed the last-minute
heroics: In the game's closing moments, with the Jets ahead
32–29, NBC preempted the contest with the children's special
Heidi. Needless to say, it was a great occasion for outcry.

Q In what round of the 1979 NFL draft was Joe Montana drafted by the San Francisco Forty-Niners?

A In the third round. Montana was the 82nd pick overall.

Q Which National Hockey League (NHL) team has won the most Stanley Cup championships?

A The Montreal Canadiens, with 23 championships.

Q Who is the holder of the most of the scoring records in the NHL?

A Wayne Gretzky, who played from 1979 to 1999, finished his career holding or sharing 61 NHL records, including the most goals scored in a season, and most goals scored in a career.

Q What is the continental divide and where is it?

A The continental divide is the drainage divide separating rivers flowing towards the opposite sides of a continent. In the United States, the Continental Divide follows the crest of the Rocky Mountains. West of the divide, the waters empty into the Pacific; east of the divide, river waters eventually flow into the Atlantic, sometimes via Hudson Bay or the Gulf of Mexico.

Q   Which state of the United States is the largest? Which state is the smallest?

A   Alaska is the largest with 570,374 square miles. Rhode Island is the smallest with 1,231 square miles.

Q   Match the states and their nicknames.
    Pennsylvania   Show Me State
    Idaho   Volunteer State
    Wisconsin   Magnolia State
    Mississippi   Keystone State
    Missouri   Gem State
    Tennessee   Badger State

A   Pennsylvania = The Keystone State; Idaho = The Gem State; Wisconsin = The Badger State; Mississippi = The Magnolia State; Missouri = The Show Me State; and Tennessee = The Volunteer State.

Q   Four states have capital cities named after American presidents. Can you name them?

A   The four states and their presidential capitals are: Mississippi (Jackson); Missouri (Jefferson City); Nebraska (Lincoln); and Wisconsin (Madison). Of course, hundreds of other Americans towns and cities have been named after presidents.

Q Who invented blue jeans?

A Jacob Davis, a Nevada tailor, came up with the idea of placing metal rivets on the denim at the points of strain. In 1873, he and Levi Strauss patented the process.

Q What is the southernmost state in the United States?

A Hawaii, which is located as far south as 18° 55' North, at Ka Lae, on the big island of Hawaii. Key West, Florida is the southernmost point in the 48 contiguous states, with a latitude of 24°33' N.

Q Who invented the computer mouse?

A Among Douglas C. Engelbart's two dozen patents is one for a "X-Y Position for a Display System," which is a prototype for the mouse. Although the device was invented in 1968, Engelbart's brainchild was not popularized until Apple used it in 1984.

Q Did Elisha Graves Otis invent the elevator?

A No, hoists already existed. But, in 1853, Otis invented the elevator brake so that they wouldn't fall—obviously, a necessary improvement.

Q Who was the inventor of the vacuum cleaner?

A Ives W. McGaffey devised the first vacuum cleaner in 1869. He called his crank-operated machine The Whirlwind. James Spangler of Canton Ohio invented the first functioning electric vacuum cleaner in 1907. It was built by the Hoover Company of New Berlin, Ohio, who rolled out their first electric Model O in 1908.

Q What are the opening words of the Declaration of Independence?

A "When in the Course of human Events, it becomes necessary for one People to dissolve the Political Bands which have connected them with another…"

Q Who wrote the Declaration of Independence?

A Thomas Jefferson spent eighteen days, from June 11 to June 28, 1776, drafting the Declaration of Independence. Jefferson incorporated changes suggested by Benjamin Franklin and John Adams.

Q **What is the first sentence of the Constitution of the United States of America?**

A "We the People of the United States, in Order to form a more perfect Union, establish Justice, insure domestic Tranquility, provide for the common defence, promote the general Welfare, and secure the Blessings of Liberty to ourselves and our Posterity, do ordain and establish this Constitution for the United States of America."

Q **What are the opening words of Abraham Lincoln's Gettysburg Address?**

A Given November 19, 1863, on the battlefield near Gettysburg, Pennsylvania: "Four score and seven years ago, our fathers brought forth upon this continent a new nation: conceived in liberty, and dedicated to the proposition that all men are created equal."

Q **What is the Nineteenth Amendment to the U.S. Constitution?**

A Adopted on August 26, 1920, the Nineteenth Amendment gives women the right to vote. "The right of citizens of the United States to vote shall not be denied or abridged by the United States or any State on account of sex."

Q What was the Eighteenth Amendment, and when was it passed?

A The Eighteenth Amendment, which was adopted on January 29, 1919, prohibited the manufacture, sale, importation, and exportation of intoxicating liquors. Prohibition was repealed by the Twenty-First Amendment, which was adopted on December 5, 1933.

Q How many voting members are there in the United States House of Representatives? How many Senators are there in the U.S. Congress?

A There are 435 voting members of the U.S. House of Representatives; in addition, there are non-voting delegates from the District of Columbia, Guam, American Samoa, the Virgin Islands, as well as a resident commissioner from Puerto Rico. The U.S. Senate has one hundred Senators.

Q How many senators does each state have in the United States Senate? How many years are there in a Senator's term?

A There are two senators from each state; each is elected for a term of six years.

Q How many members of the U.S. House of Representatives does each state have?

A Population determines the number of representatives per state in the House of Representatives. The numbers of representatives per state ranges from one in states with lower populations to fifty-two representatives in California.

Q Which seven states have only one representative in the United States House of Representatives?

A Alaska, Delaware, Montana, North Dakota, South Dakota, Vermont, and Wyoming have only one member of the United States House of Representatives.

Q Was it P. T. Barnum who said, "there's a sucker born every minute"?

A Although he was known for being a shameless huckster, there is no proof that he actually made that remark. In addition to his famous circus, Barnum was the showman who first presented to America the Cardiff Giant, Tom Thumb, and the original Siamese twins, Chang and Eng. He began his career hawking an elderly, blind African-American woman as being the 161-year-old former nurse of George Washington.

Q Did P. T. Barnum ever serve in an elected office?

A Phineas Taylor Barnum was elected to the Connecticut state legislature in 1865. He had also served as the mayor of Bridgeport, Connecticut.

Q What movie character was famous for saying, "What's up, Doc?"

A Bugs Bunny. Frederick Bean "Tex" Avery (1908–1980) was Bugs's creator, and Mel Blanc (1908–1989) was the voice.

Q When did Porky Pig make his first movie?

A On March 2, 1935, Porky Pig appeared in his first film, *I Haven't Got a Hat*, directed by Friz Freleng. Porky's career developed alongside the career of Warner Brothers's head of animation Chuck Jones. Porky's best-known line is "Th-th-th-that's all, folks!"

Q What are the names of the seven diminutive people in Walt Disney's *Snow White and the Seven Dwarfs*?

A In Walt Disney's 1937 adaptation of the old fairy tale, the forest-dwelling dwarfs have the names of Dopey, Sneezy, Grumpy, Happy, Bashful, Doc, and Sleepy.

Q Where did Walt Disney's seven dwarfs work?

A They worked in the mines, digging for diamonds. They sang "Heigh-ho" on their way to and from the mines. They also liked to whistle while they worked.

Q What is the name of the well-known singing group that signed with Motown Records in 1969, and hails from Gary, Indiana? What are the first names of the members of this group?

A The Jackson Five. Jackie (born Sigmund), Tito (born Toriano), Jermaine, Marlon, and Michael.

Q What singer was called the "Chairman of the Board"?

A Frank Sinatra, also known as "Old Blue Eyes."

Q What was the biggest hit by the soul group named The Chairmen of the Board?

A Although The Chairmen of the Board had a few minor hits, their biggest chartbuster was their debut single, "Give Me Just A Little More Time," released in 1970 on Invicta Records.

Q **Which father and daughter combination had a top 40 hit singing a duet?**

A Only one father and daughter combination qualifies as producing a solid Top 40 hit singing a duet: Frank Sinatra and Nancy Sinatra had a big hit in 1967, "Something Stupid." There are two other recordings that could be considered, however. In 1960, Carla Thomas and her father Rufus Thomas recorded a song that was a hit in the Memphis area, "Cause I Love You." And in 1991, Natalie Cole sang a tribute "duet" with her late father, Nat "King"Cole, by recording her voice track with his original recording of "Unforgettable."

Q **What was Elvis Presley's middle name? Where was he born? Where and when did he die?**

A Elvis Aron Presley was born in Tupelo, Mississippi on January 8, 1935. Although there are those who believe otherwise, the general opinion is that that he died at the age of 42 at his home, Graceland, in Memphis, on August 16, 1977.

Q **What was Elvis's profession before he became famous as a rock and roll singer?**

A Elvis was a truck driver in Memphis.

Q Is Elvis's middle name misspelled on his tombstone?

A Yes. Elvis's full name is Elvis Aron Presley, but on his grave his middle name is spelled incorrectly as "Aaron," with two a's. People who believe Elvis is not dead point to this fact as part of the evidence of a conspiracy.

Q How many movies were Elvis Presley and Nancy Sinatra in together?

A Just one—the easy-to-forget *Speedway* (1968), directed by Norman Taurog. Elvis plays Steve Grayson, a stock car racer who owes the Internal Revenue Service hundreds of thousands of dollars, due to bad accounting practices by his accountant, played by Bill Bixby. Nancy Sinatra plays an IRS agent who is supposed to collect the money.

Q What recording company released the first recordings of Elvis Presley?

A Sun Records, Sam Phillips's little Memphis music company, pressed the first Elvis Presley records in 1954. "That's All Right, Mama" was on the hit side.

Q What did Michael Jackson say just before he passionately kissed his then-wife Lisa Marie Presley onstage at the MTV Video Music Awards on September 8, 1994?

A "And just think, nobody thought this would last." However, Presley and Jackson were divorced by 1996. Their marriage lasted 20 months—from May 1994 to January 1996.

Q What was the date of the launch of the world's first artificial satellite?

A The Soviet Union launched the communications satellite *Sputnik* into orbit on October 4, 1957. The immediate response in the United States was putting out several records with "sputnik" in the lyrics.

Q When did the United States launch its first satellite?

A The first United States satellite was the *Explorer I* on Jan. 31, 1958, almost four months after *Sputnik*.

Q What was the name of the first human sent into space?

A Soviet cosmonaut Yuri Gagarin became the first human in space on April 12, 1961. His *Vostok I* spacecraft orbited the earth once.

Q What was the name of the first American sent into space?

A On May 5, 1961, astronaut Alan B. Shepard, Jr. became the first American in space in a 15 minute, 28 second sub-orbital flight. John H. Glenn, Jr. became the first U.S. astronaut to orbit the Earth in 1962.

Q Who was the first woman in space?

A Velentina Tereshkova became the first woman to travel in space. She made 45 revolutions of the earth in the spacecraft *Vostok 6* on June 16–19, 1963. The first American woman in space was Sally Ride, who made her first trip aboard the shuttle *Challenger* on June 18–24, 1983.

Q Who was the first man on the moon?

A At 10:56 PM EDT, July 20, 1969, American astronaut Neil Armstrong became the first person to set foot on the Moon. Armstrong and Edwin "Buzz" Aldrin left the *Eagle* lunar landing module for more than two hours during which time they played a little golf, and rode around in the lunar buggy. Meanwhile, astronaut Michael Collins orbited the moon in the Command module.

Q What were Armstrong's first words when he first stood on the moon's surface?

A "That's one small step for [a] man, one giant leap for Mankind."

Q Where is the lunar buggy now?

A Still on the moon. Luckily, the moon has free parking.

Q Who was the first president of the United States who was born an American citizen?

A Martin Van Buren was the first chief executive born in this country after the Declaration of Independence. All previous American presidents had been born as British subjects.

Q For one president, English was not his mother tongue. Name the president and his first language.

A Martin Van Buren grew up speaking Dutch, the first language of his parents.

Q Who popularized the expression "O.K."?

A There are several theories about thee origin of the expression "O.K.," but one thing is certain: Supporters of Martin Van Buren called their favorite candidate "O.K.," for "Old Kinderhook." Van Buren's nickname derived from Kinderhook, New York, his place of birth.

Q Who was the youngest person to win an acting Oscar?

A Tatum O'Neal won a Best Supporting Actress award for the 1973 film *Paper Moon* when she was 10.
Shirley Temple had been given an honorary "Special Oscar" at the age of 5 in 1934, but it was not in a competitive category.

Q Who is the oldest person to win an acting Oscar?

A Jessica Tandy won the Best Actress award for *Driving Miss Daisy* (1989) at age 81.

Q Who has won the Best Supporting Actor award the most times?

A Walter Brennan, who won three times for the films *Come and Get It* (1936), *Kentucky* (1938), and *The Westerner* (1940).

Q Who is the only person to win an Academy Award for playing a member of the opposite sex?

A Linda Hunt won the Best Supporting Actress Oscar for *The Year of Living Dangerously* (1983). In the movie she plays a man named Billy Kwan.

Q Name the first actor or actress to win an Academy Award for a performance that was entirely not in English.

A Sophia Loren won Best Actress for her role in the Italian language film *Two Women* (1961).

Q The shower scene in the 1960 classic *Psycho* is one of the most famous in film history. Name the character killed in the shower scene and the actress who played her. For bonus points, name the city in which the movie's opening scenes occur.

A Marion Crane was played by Janet Leigh. She lived in Phoenix, Arizona.

Q In the 2001 movie *A Beautiful Mind* (and real life too, for that matter), in what field did John Nash win a Nobel Prize?

A Economics (in 1994).

Q What director said, "I demand that a film express either the joy of making cinema or the agony of making cinema; I am not at all interested in anything in between; I am not interested in all those films that do not pulse."

A François Truffaut, who directed such films as *Two English Girls* (1972) and *Day For Night* (1973).

Q In the original 1970s television series, what actresses played the angels of Charlie?

A Kate Jackson, Farrah Fawcett, and Jaclyn Smith were the original lineup. Cheryl Ladd, Shelley Hack, and Tanya Roberts were later replacements.

Q Who was the lead in the *Six Million Dollar Man* (1974–1978)?

A Lee Majors (then married to Farrah Fawcett) played Colonel Steve Austin, the test pilot who had the expensive replacement implants.

Q *Maude* and *The Jeffersons* both share the distinction of being spinoffs from the same show. What show?

A *All in the Family*. The show lasted from 1971 to 1979.

Q Another *All in the Family* question: What was Meathead's full name?

A Michael Stivic. He was played by Rob Reiner. The show lasted from 1971–1979.

Q What business was George Jefferson in that enabled him to "move on up"?

A On the sitcom *The Jeffersons* (1975–1985), George owned several dry cleaning stores.

Q What is the largest island in the world?

A The island of Greenland, in the North Atlantic Ocean, is the world's largest island, covering 840,000 square miles. Greenland is a dependency of Denmark. The island of Australia is larger than Greenland, but it is considered a continent.

Q What is the largest continent in the world?

A Measuring more than seventeen million square miles, Asia is nearly one-third of the earth's landmass, and, by far, the largest continent.

Q Is the continent of Europe part of the continent of Asia?

A Europe could be considered a large peninsula of the continent of Asia; some geographers refer to the landmass as "Eurasia."

Q How large is the United States in relation to the continent of Africa?

A The United States would fit into the continent of Africa three-and-a-half times.

Q Where is the Gobi Desert?

A The Gobi Desert is a desert and semidesert region of Central Asia stretching across the Mongolian People's Republic and the Inner Mongolia region of China. Its total area is about 500,000 square miles.

Q What percentage of the world's land surface is desert?

A Twenty to twenty-five percent.

Q Who was the shortest American president?

A James Madison stood only 5'4". He was probably the lightest American president in history, too: He weighed in at only a hundred pounds.

Q Who was the tallest American president?

A Easy. Abraham Lincoln was 6'4".

Q In which U.S. state was Confederate President Jefferson Davis born?

A Jefferson Davis was born on June 3, 1808 in Christian County, Kentucky. His birthplace is now the Jefferson Davis Historic Site administered by the state of Kentucky. Not so far away, in Hardin County, Kentucky, Abraham Lincoln was born on February 12, 1809. His birthplace is now the Abraham Lincoln Birthplace National Historic Site.

Q What is the name of Ashley Wilkes' plantation in *Gone With the Wind*?

A Ashley, played by Leslie Howard, owns "Twelve Oaks."

Q Victor Fleming won the 1939 Academy Award for Best Director for *Gone With the Wind*, which also won Best Picture. Fleming directed another movie nominated for Best Picture that year. Name it.

A *The Wizard of Oz.*

Q Who played Dorothy in the 1978 film version of *The Wiz*? Who played The Scarecrow?

A Diana Ross played Dorothy, and none other than pop star Michael Jackson played The Scarecrow.

Q Who were the world's first surfers?

A Captain James Cook was the first European to visit the Hawaiian Islands in 1778. When he arrived, riding the ocean waves on a narrow surfboard was already a popular sport in Hawaii.

Q What name was Hawaii given when the Europeans discovered it?

A In 1778, English Captain Cook named the islands we now call Hawaii the Sandwich Islands, for the Earl of Sandwich.

Q Where did the sandwich get its name?

A John Montagu, the Fourth Earl of Sandwich (1718–1792), was a British nobleman who served as the Secretary of State and First Lord of the Admiralty, and is credited with popularizing the idea of sandwiches. He loved to gamble, and hated to leave the gaming table. Having meat served between two slices of bread allowed the Earl to eat while he stayed in the game. Soon, this way of serving food was named after him.

Q What is the latitude of the equator?

A 0°. The equator is a great circle around the earth that has a latitude of zero degrees. It is the base line from which latitude is calculated over the globe. The equator is equidistant from the two geographical poles, dividing the earth into the northern and southern hemispheres.

Q What is the longitude of the prime meridian?

A 0°. The prime meridian has a longitude of zero degrees and runs through Greenwich, England. It separates the east and west longitudes.

Q What is the International Date Line?

A The International Date Line, halfway round the earth from Greenwich, roughly following the 180° meridian, is the line where each calendar day begins. The date on the western side of the line (in the Eastern Hemisphere) is one day later than the date on the eastern side of the line (in the Western Hemisphere).

Q When a new London Bridge was built in 1973, the bridge built in 1831 was taken down. Where is it now?

A The London Bridge that was built in 1831 is now in Lake Havasu City, Arizona. It used to cross the Thames River in London, England. The 1831 bridge, designed by John Rennie, was itself a replacement for the medieval London Bridge of nursery rhyme fame.

Q Where is the Ponte Vecchio?

A Considered to be an outstanding engineering achievement of the Italian Middle Ages, the Ponte Vecchio is a much-photographed bridge that crosses over the Arno River at Florence.

Q Why is the bridge in Venice named the "Bridge of Sighs"?

A The "Bridge of Sighs" received its nickname in the seventeenth century, inspired by the sighs of prisoners as they were led over the bridge on their way to the prison cells. This bridge over the Rio di Palazzo, built in 1600, connected the prisons to the inquisitor's rooms in the main palace.

Q In 1940, what was the nickname for the Tacoma Narrows Bridge across Puget Sound?

A The Tacoma Narrows Bridge was nicknamed "Galloping Gertie" because, on November 7, 1940, just four months after the bridge's opening, the deck twisted, rolled, and buckled under a wind of 42 miles per hour. Needless to say, the bridge had engineering and design problems. The Tacoma Narrows Bridge was replaced in 1950 by a new span.

Q When was indoor plumbing installed in the White House?

A During the administration of Millard Fillmore, at Mrs. Fillmore's insistence.

Q What White House fixture had to be replaced during William Howard Taft's term?

A A new and larger bathtub was installed after the 332-pound Taft became hopelessly stuck while taking an executive bath. It is said that it took six men to extricate the embarrassed Commander in Chief.

Q During which administration were electric lights added to the White House?

A During Benjamin Harrison's, in 1891.

Q Who made the first presidential phone call?

A Rutherford B. Hayes had a telephone in the White House in 1879.

Q On June 2nd, 1886, a historic event occurred at the White House. What was it?

A That day, for the first and only time, a U.S. President was married in the White House: Grover Cleveland married Frances Folsom in the Blue Room.

Q Which president had a pet parrot named "Washington Post"?

A President William McKinley. The parrot that belonged to McKinley, the 25th president of the United States, reportedly could whistle "Yankee Doodle." Other presidential parrot owners include Andrew Jackson, Ulysses S. Grant, the Madisons, and the first First Lady, Martha Washington.

Q Who was president when a leg of a piano went through the floor of the White House?

A In 1948, when Harry S Truman was president, a leg of his piano punched a hole in the floor.

Q How many rooms are there in today's White House? How many bathrooms?

A 132 rooms, 35 bathrooms. Also, 412 doors, 147 windows, 28 fireplaces, eight staircases, and three elevators.

Q What songs did President Ulysses S. Grant claim to know?

A Ulysses S. Grant once remarked about his musical knowledge: "I know only two tunes—one is Yankee Doodle and the other isn't."

Q Who was Patrick Henry? What is his famous quote?

A Patrick Henry was a famous orator, an influential statesman, and governor of Virginia at the time of the American Revolution. He is best known for saying "Give me liberty or give me death!" at a convention in 1775. He was referring to taking up the cause of arming the militia.

Q Who were Mason and Dixon? What is the Mason-Dixon Line?

A In 1763, Charles Mason and Jeremiah Dixon were commissioned by the heirs of William Penn and Lord Baltimore to settle an old boundary dispute between Pennsylvania and Maryland. Proceeding along the parallel of latitude 39° 43' 20" N, their work was limited to the two states of Pennsylvania and Maryland. Later, the Mason and Dixon Line became known as the boundary between free states and slave states, and is now regarded as the boundary between the North and the South.

Q When was gold first discovered in the Yukon?

A On August 17, 1896, three men (Skookum Jim, Tagish Charlie, and American George Carmack) discovered gold in Rabbit Creek, which they renamed Bonanza Creek. The 1898 Klondike Gold Rush was on. Over 100,000 adventurers arrived over the next few years.

Q Who were Marbury and Madison, litigants in the well-known case before the Supreme Court?

A William Marbury sued Secretary of State James Madison to force him to deliver his commission as a justice of the peace. Under the Judiciary Act of 1800, a number of new judgeships had been created; although Marbury had been appointed, he was not formally commissioned (or paid). The importance of the case is that, in ruling, Supreme Court Chief Justice John Marshall established the judicial right to review the constitutionality of legislation.

Q What was the path of the Oregon Trail? What was its significance?

A The Oregon Trail ran about 2,000 miles, from Independence, Missouri, to the Columbia River region in Oregon. The Trail generally follows the Platte River to its headwaters, then crosses the mountains, and then follows the Snake River to the Columbia River. It was a trail first used by fur traders and missionaries, but, beginning in 1842, wagon trains kicked off a massive move west on the Oregon Trail. More than 500,000 people traveled west on the Trail over the next twenty-five years, until the transcontinental railroad was completed in 1869.

Q How long did it take Robert Fulton's steamship to make the trip from New York City to Albany, New York?

A Beginning on August 17, 1807, Robert Fulton made the first practical steamboat trip, a 150 mile voyage from New York City to Albany, in 32 hours.

Q How many immigrants passed through Ellis Island?

A Twenty-two million people passed through Ellis Island, which is situated in New York Harbor, in its years of operation as the United States's principal immigration reception center from 1892 to 1924.

Q How did the bazooka gun get its name?

A As unusual as it sounds, the armor-piercing hollow-tube weapon developed during WW2 was named after the humorous musical instrument that radio entertainer Bob Burns had fashioned from two gas pipes and a funnel.

Q On *Cheers* (1982–1993), Norm's wife is often referred to but never fully seen. What was her name?

A Vera.

Q What was the name of Bob Burns's radio show?

A Bob Burns had a radio show that was popular in the '30s and '40s, called *The Arkansas Traveler.* His show has been described as a precursor to *Hee-Haw.*

Q What was the "Monkey Trial"? Was the accused found guilty?

A In 1925, John T. Scopes, a 24-year old biology teacher, was put on trial in Dayton, Tennessee for illegally teaching evolution to high school students, a violation of the Butler Act. The trial became a major media event, and the lawyers were Williams Jennings Bryan for the prosecution and Clarence Darrow for the defense. Scopes was found guilty and fined one hundred dollars. The conviction was later overturned by the Tennessee Supreme Court.

Q Who played the Incredible Hulk in the 1978–1982 series?

A Lou Ferrigno played the Incredible Hulk, and Bill Bixby was scientist Dr. Banner, during his calmer periods.

Q Barney Miller worked at police precinct full of funny characters. What was the name of the precinct?

A The 12th Precinct. *Barney Miller* aired from 1975–1982.

Q Why is thoroughbred horse racing called "the sport of kings"?

A Because the royalty was interested in thoroughbred racing. As early as 1110, England's King Henry I had imported an Arabian stallion from Spain, and horse racing became a favorite pastime of the English royalty and nobility.

In the mid-1600s, King Charles II of England was a racing enthusiast and did much to revive the popularity of the sport.

Q What is the Triple Crown in U.S. thoroughbred horse racing?

A The three major U.S. races for horses three years of age—the Kentucky Derby, the Preakness Stakes, and the Belmont Stakes—comprise the Triple Crown. The last Triple Crown winner was Affirmed, who out-dueled Alydar in all three races in 1978.

Q How does a batter win the Triple Crown in baseball? Who was the last person to win it?

A In baseball, the batter who leads the league in batting average, home runs, and RBIs is the winner of the Triple Crown. The last winner of the Triple Crown in baseball was Carl Yastrzemski of the Boston Red Sox in 1967.

Q When did the Yankees first wear pinstripes?

A On April 11, 1912, pinstripes first appeared on the uniforms of the Highlanders, who were the forerunners of the New York Yankees.

Q In what cities did the baseball Braves make their home before they moved to Atlanta?

A Boston and Milwaukee. Before they were the Atlanta Braves, they were the Boston Red Stockings (1876–1883), the Boston Beaneaters (1883–1907), the Boston Doves (1908–1912), the Boston Braves (1913–1952) before they moved to Milwaukee, where they played from 1953 to 1965. In 1966, the Braves became the Atlanta Braves.

Q **When was the spitball made illegal in major league baseball?**

A In 1920, major league baseball banned the spitball, but allowed all the pitchers currently throwing it at the time to continue to do so. When pitcher Burleigh Grimes retired in 1934 (with 270 wins), the legal spitball was dead.

Q **When was the first World Series played?**

A Although there had been other post-season championships played as early as 1884, the first World Series Championship was played in 1903. The Pittsburgh Pirates and the Boston Pilgrims (later the Red Sox) met in a best-of-nine-game post-season series in September 1903. Boston upset the favored Pirates, five games to three.

Q **What was the "Black Sox scandal" of 1919?**

A In the most famous scandal in baseball history, eight players from the Chicago White Sox (later scorned as the Black Sox) were accused of throwing the World Series against the Cincinnati Reds. The players involved were banned from professional baseball for life.

Q When was the first telecast of a major league baseball game?

A In the first major league baseball telecast on August 26, 1939, the Brooklyn Dodgers split a doubleheader with the Cincinnati Reds at Ebbets Field, Brooklyn, broadcast on W2XBS, the RCA station in New York.

Q For what activity is baseball player Moe Berg best-known?

A As a player, Moe Berg was only a journeyman infielder/catcher who had a .243 lifetime batting average over his sixteen-year career. But, Moe Berg was also a spy for the Americans. Among other things, in 1934, while touring Japan with a team that included Babe Ruth, he took photographs of Tokyo that helped guide American bombers during the war.

Q Why do baseball managers wear uniforms?

A It's the rules. Only people in uniforms are allowed on the field during play. Baseball managers and coaches almost always wear the team uniforms, but at least one manager, Connie Mack (1862-1956), wore a business suit. He had to send his coaches out on the field.

Q How many bones are there in the human body?

A Adult humans have 206 bones. Surprisingly, babies have more bones than grown-ups. As the child matures, bones fuse together.

Q Where do you find the bones that have the nicknames of the hammer, anvil, and stirrup? What important role do they play in the human body?

A These bones, formally known as the malleus, incus, and stapes, are three small bones located in the ear canal and are called the ossicles. They are essential to the hearing process; they vibrate in a chain reaction and conduct sound waves through the middle ear.

Q What is the smallest bone in the human body?

A The stapes, a.k.a. the stirrup.

Q What famous movie is about a revolt started by Russian sailors in 1905?

A Sergei Eisenstein's *The Battleship Potemkin* (1925).

Q Malapropism is the incorrect use of a word which sounds similar to the correct one. This term comes from a character in an eighteenth century play. What is the name of the character and the name of the play?

A Mrs. Malaprop, a character in Richard Brinsley Sheridan's 1775 comedy, *The Rivals*. Malaprops often provoke laughter—sometimes intentionally, sometimes not.

Q What were the two aspects of William Henry Harrison's 1841 inaugural address that made it historic?

A First, it was the longest inaugural address in presidential history: One hour and forty minutes. Second, it probably killed him. Although he was sixty-eight years and noticeably frail, Harrison insisted on delivering his lengthy address without hat, gloves, or overcoat. The combination of the brisk March weather and a downpour took its toll. Harrison became ill and never recovered. He died exactly a month after his inaugural.

Q Who had the campaign slogan "Tippecanoe and Tyler too"?

A 9th President William Henry Harrison, who led troops in the military victory over Shawnee Chief Tecumseh at The Battle of Tippecanoe (1811). John Tyler was his V-P running mate.

Q Which U.S. president joined the Confederacy after he was no longer in office?

A Virginian John Tyler was elected as a delegate to the Congress of the Confederacy in 1861 but he died before he could take his seat. This rebellious deed won him an unprecedented silence: His death, unlike those of all his predecessors, was not announced by the White House.

Q Who famously said, "My country, right or wrong"?

A Stephen Decatur. Actually, in his original 1816 statement, Decatur said "our country," not "my country." The relevant quotation is "Our country! In her intercourse with foreign nations, may she always be in the right; but our country, right or wrong."

Q Where is the Liberty Bell?

A The Liberty Bell is housed at 6th and Chestnut Streets in Philadelphia's Liberty Bell Center, which is part of Independence National Historical Park. One of the most famous symbols of the battle for American independence, the Liberty Bell was rung on July 8, 1776 to summon the public to hear a reading of the Declaration of Independence.

Q As a naval commander, Stephen Decatur fought heroically in the Tripolitan War, the Algerine War, and the War of 1812. How did this heroic warrior die?

A Ironically, after surviving numerous bloody naval battles, Decatur died at the hands of a fellow American military leader. Early in his career, he served as a judge at the court-martial that convicted Commodore James Barron. After Decatur repeatedly resisted the commodore's attempts at reinstatement, Barron challenged him to a duel. On March 22, 1820, the two met on the field and exchange gunfire. Both were wounded, Decatur mortally.

Q What 1961 film included the last appearances of both Clark Gable and Marilyn Monroe?

A *The Misfits*, which had a screenplay by Monroe's ex-husband, Arthur Miller.

Q At the end of *Annie Hall* (1977), what actress plays the role of Woody Allen's date?

A Sigourney Weaver.

Q Who garnered the Oscar for Best Adapted Screenplay for *The Bridge on the River Kwai* **(1957) and what's significant about this win?**

A Pierre Boulle had written the original novel *The Bridge on the River Kwai* in French and was given credit for the screenplay, even though he did not work on the screenplay at all. In fact Boulle could not write in English. Years later the credit was changed to the real authors of the script— blacklisted writers Michael Wilson and Carl Foreman.

Q What was Rick's last name in *Casablanca?*

A Rick Blaine was the character played by Humphrey Bogart. Ingrid Bergman played Ilsa Lund Laszlo.

Q Did the film *Casablanca* **win an Oscar?**

A Yes, it won three Academy Awards in 1943, including Best Picture. It also won Oscars for Best Director for Michael Curtiz, and Best Screenplay for Julius and Philip Epstein and Howard Koch.

Q What is the title of the play that *Casablanca* is based on?

A *Everybody Comes to Rick's*, written by Murray Bernett and Joan Alison.

Q When was Apple Computer founded?

A On April 1, 1976, Steven Wozniak and Steven Jobs, who had been friends in high school, founded the Apple Computer Company. Both had been working in Silicon Valley, California when Wozniak designed what would become the first Apple computer.

Q When was U.S. Steel founded?

A The United States Steel Corporation was formed in 1901. At that time, it was the largest business enterprise ever launched. U.S. Steel was the first billion-dollar enterprise in American history.

Q What was the Burma Road?

A The Burma Road was a 700 mile long road built during World War Two, leading from Lashio, Burma to Kunming, China. It was used by the Allies for transporting supplies to China for use against Japan.

Q How many miles of public roads are there in the U.S.?

A There are estimated to be over four million miles of public roads in the United States, enough to circle the globe 150 times.

Q What is the origin of the term "maverick"?

A Samuel A. Maverick (1803–1870) was a Texas pioneer who did not brand his calves. Maverick's herd was allowed to wander and gave rise to the term *maverick*, which denotes a stray, unbranded calf. Today, the word also refers to a person who refuses to go along with the crowd.

Q Who invented the guillotine?

A The guillotine was invented by French doctor Joseph Guillotin (1738–1814), who argued for a quick, painless method of capital punishment. Doctor Guillotin worked together with German engineer Tobias Schmidt to build a prototype guillotine machine, with the blade at an oblique 45-degree angle. The first guillotining took place on April 25, 1792. Thousands of people were guillotined during the French Revolution.

Q Most people know that an iceberg sunk the Titanic, but do you know what sent these vessels to the bottom of the sea?

a) *R.M.S. Lusitania*   d) *S.S. Edmund Fitzgerald*

b) *U.S.S. Monitor*   e) *The Andrea Doria*

c) *C.S.S. Virginia*

A a) A torpedo from a German U-boat sank this passenger ship on May 7, 1915.

b) This ironclad survived its battle with the Merrimack, but was lost in a storm off Cape Hatteras on December 31, 1862

c) To prevent its capture by Union forces, this Confederate ironclad was scuttled on May 11, 1862.

d) This 729-foot freighter and its 29-man crew were lost in a storm on Lake Superior on November 10, 1975.

e) On July 26, 1956, this giant passenger ship sunk after a collision with the cruise ship *Stockholm*.

Q What letters are the most valuable letters in *Scrabble®*?

A The letters "Q" and "Z" are each worth 10 points. "J" and "X" are worth 8 each.

Q In the film *Casablanca*, who played and sang the song "As Time Goes By"?

A Dooley Wilson was Sam, who played it again. The 1942 film starred Humphrey Bogart and Ingrid Bergman.

Q Match the capital cities and the countries.

Canada	Budapest
Hungary	Wellington
New Zealand	Nicosia
Tanzania	Ottawa
Cyprus	Dar-Es-Salaam
Pakistan	Islamabad

A Canada—Ottawa, Hungary—Budapest, New Zealand— Wellington, Tanzania—Dar-Es-salaam, Cyprus—Nicosia, Pakistan—Islamabad.

Q On September 23, 2005, at a special concert at the Hollywood Bowl, which movie scores were revealed as the top five of all time by the American Film Institute?

A 1. *Star Wars* (1977) John Williams, 2. *Gone With the Wind* (1939) Max Steiner, 3. *Lawrence of Arabia* (1962) Maurice Jarre, 4. *Psycho* (1960) Bernard Herrmann, and 5. *The Godfather* (1972) Nino Rota.

Q *Invasion of the Body Snatchers* (1956), *Flaming Star* (1960, with Elvis) and *Dirty Harry* (1971) were all directed by the same man, who had already won an Oscar for short subject direction. Can you name him?

A Don Siegel (1912-1991).

Q What are the top five movie songs, according to a poll of jurors from the American Film Institute (AFI)? What are the names of the composers?

A 1. "Over the Rainbow" (*The Wizard of Oz*, 1939) music/lyrics: Harold Arlen/E. Y. Harburg
2. "As Time Goes By" (*Casablanca*, 1942) music/lyrics: Herman Hupfeld
3. "Singin' in the Rain" (*Singin' in the Rain*, 1952) music/lyrics: Nacio Herb Brown/Arthur Freed
4. "Moon River" (*Breakfast at Tiffany's*, 1961 music/lyrics: Henry Mancini/Johnny Mercer
5. "White Christmas" (*Holiday Inn*, 1942) music/lyrics: Irving Berlin

The American Film Institute announced the top movie songs of all time on a three-hour TV special hosted by John Travolta. Travolta was not only the host of the show, his career includes his performance in *Saturday Night Fever* (1977), the film where number nine on the list, "Staying Alive" by the BeeGees, was sung.

Q When did Alexander the Great live?

A Alexander the Great was born in 356 B.C.E. He was the King of Macedonia who conquered much of the ancient world from Asia Minor to Egypt and India. Alexander is considered a military genius. He died in 323 B.C.E.

Q As part of the American Film Institute's 100 Years celebration, the top movie heroes and top movie villains of all time were announced. Who was filmdom's top hero? Who was the top villain?

A Attorney Atticus Finch (portrayed by Gregory Peck), from *To Kill A Mockingbird* (1962) was chosen as the greatest hero in film history, while the greatest villain was revealed as Dr. Hannibal Lecter (portrayed by Anthony Hopkins) from *The Silence of the Lambs* (1991).

Q Who were the Celts?

A Also spelled *Kelt*, the Celts were an early Indo-European people who migrated over much of Europe from the 2nd millennium B.C.E. to the 1st century B.C.E. They ranged from the British Isles and northern Spain to as far east as the Black Sea. The native speakers of Ireland, Scotland, Wales, the Isle of Man, and Brittany all speak Celtic languages.

Q In 1914, the Russian city of St. Petersburg was renamed. What was the city's name during the First World War?

A Petrograd. The Russians decided that the name of St. Petersburg, founded in 1703, was too German-sounding, so they renamed it Petrograd. In 1924, the Soviets renamed it Leningrad, after Vladimir Lenin. In 1991, it was named St. Petersburg once again.

Q What is a Gordian knot?

A In Greek mythology, Gordius, king of Phrygia, tied a knot so intricate that no one could undo it. An oracle has said that the one to undo it will be the future ruler of Asia. When Alexander the Great was unable to untie the Gordian knot, he cut it through with one stroke of his sword, thereby solving a perplexing problem by a simple, decisive action. He had cut the Gordian knot.

Q Who were the Druids?

A No one knows exactly, but it is believed that the Druids were the priests of the ancient Celtic people. They filled the roles of priests, scholars, teachers, and judges in Celtic society. It is believed that the stone circles found in Britain, the most well known being Stonehenge, are associated with the Druids. The earliest known records of the Druids come from. the third century B.C.E.

Q In what movie did Johnny Depp make his film debut?

A Johnny Depp's first film role was playing a character named Glen Lantz in *A Nightmare on Elm Street* in 1984. This film also introduced the character of Freddie Krueger, played by John Englund.

Q Where was the Battle of Bunker Hill fought? When?

A The Battle of Bunker Hill was actually fought on Breed's Hill, Massachusetts, on June 17, 1775. The British troops under the command of General Howe, were ordered to charge the position held by the American Patriots on Breed's Hill. On their third attempt to take the hill, the Americans were forced to retreat. Although it was a British victory, the battle showed the patriots that the British were not invincible, encouraging the Patriot cause.

Q Did German U-boats land in the United States during the Second World War?

A Yes, the Germans landed U-boats on New York's Long Island, and in Florida. Four German agents were put ashore at each location with instructions to destroy American factories. The agents from the Long Island landing were spotted right away, and the FBI was soon hot on the trail. One of the German agents turned himself in, and the FBI was able to round up the rest of the agents.

Q On the 1990s show *Beverly Hills 90210*, the kids hung out at a local diner. What was the name of the diner?

A The Peach Pit.

Q On *Welcome Back Kotter* (1975–1979), Mr. Kotter taught a group of troubled teens. What was this group of kids called? The show was set in what part of New York?

A The Sweathogs. Brooklyn, New York. Mega-star John Travolta started his career as Sweathog Vinnie Barbarino.

Q What was the name of the suburban town where Dick Van Dyke and Mary Tyler Moore lived on the 1960s *The Dick Van Dyke Show*?

A New Rochelle, New York

Q What was the name of the show where Dick Van Dyke's character worked?

A The Alan Brady Show. Alan Brady was played by Carl Reiner.

Q What are the last names of George and Elaine on *Seinfeld* (1990-1998)? What is Kramer's first name?

A George Costanza, Elaine Benes. Cosmo Kramer.

Q   What family has had three generations of Oscar winners?

A   The Hustons. Walter Huston won Best Supporting Actor honors for *Treasure of the Sierra Madre* (1948). Walter's son, John, took home Best Director and Best Screenplay awards for the same movie. John's daughter, Angelica, won Best Supporting Actress for *Prizzi's Honor* (1985).

Q   Jack Lemmon won a Best Supporting Actor Oscar for the role of Ensign Pulver in the 1955 film *Mister Roberts*. Do you know what his improbable, official shipboard job title was?

A   Laundry and Morale Officer.

Q   Where is the world's longest underground cave system?

A   The cave system in Kentucky's Mammoth Cave National Park is the world's longest cave system. Mammoth Cave connects to the Flint Ridge cave system—the explored and mapped underground passages have a combined length of more than 365 miles.

Q **Is it stalactites or stalagmites that hang from the ceiling of caves?**

A Icicle-shaped stalactites, which are formed by ground water dripping, hang from the ceiling. One handy tip is that the letter "c" in stalactite stands for the ceiling, and the "g" in stalagmite is for the structure that sticks up from the ground. Sometimes, the two calcites meet and form solid pillars.

Q **Who was Floyd Collins?**

A In 1925, Floyd Collins, then considered to be one of the world's top spelunkers, was trapped by a falling rock in Kentucky's Sand Cave. He was wedged in, 150 feet below the surface, and ended up dying after being trapped for fifteen days. The new medium of radio brought the unfolding story of the attempted rescue to the living rooms of the whole country.

Q **What is the Chinook wind?**

A The Chinooks are the warm dry winds that flow down from the eastern slopes of the Rocky Mountains and have been known to raise temperatures by 30 degrees Fahrenheit in only a few hours.

Q What is the strongest recorded earthquake in history?

A The strongest recorded earthquake was in Chile in 1960—
the magnitude was 9.5 on the Richter scale. The main shock
set up a series of seismic sea waves that caused extensive
damage as far away as Hawaii and Japan. The next strongest
earthquake was at Prince William Sound in Alaska in
1964—9.2. It is also the most severe earthquake in United
States history.

**Q What was the largest earthquake in the history of 48
contiguous United States?**

A On February 7, 1812, there was an earthquake with a
magnitude of at least 7.9 in New Madrid, Missouri.

Q What is the world's largest active volcano?

A The most massive volcano in the world is Mauna Loa in
Hawaii, at 13,677 feet. Its dome is 75 miles long and 64
miles wide, and its lava flows occupy more than 2,000 square
miles. Mauna Loa averages one eruption every 3½ years.

Q What is the southernmost land on Earth?

A The land of Antarctica, at the South Pole, is the southernmost land on Earth.

Q What is the northernmost land on Earth?

A Unlike the South Pole, the North Pole is on an ice pack, not on land. The northernmost land is Cape Morris Jessup, Greenland, with a latitude of approximately 84° North.

Q Match the *Batman* (1966–1968) TV villain with the actor who played him or her.

1. Egghead　　　　　A. Caesar Romero
2. The Riddler　　　　B. Vincent Price
3. The Joker　　　　　C. Frank Gorshin
4. The Penguin　　　　D. Burgess Meredith

A 1. The Egghead – B. Vincent Price;
2. The Riddler – C. Frank Gorshin;
3. The Joker – A. Caesar Romero;
4 The Penguin – D. Burgess Meredith

Q Rick Shroeder played a cop on *NYPD Blue* (1993–2005). What was the name of the sitcom he starred in as a kid?

A *Silver Spoons* (1982–1987). He was called "Ricky" back then.

Q Who was the first woman to be elected governor of a state?

A Nellie Tayloe Ross of Wyoming was the nation's first woman governor. She won a special election in 1924 to complete her deceased husband's term.

Q Which state was the first to give women the right to vote?

A In 1869, Wyoming, which was still a territory, gave women the right to vote. Wyoming became a state in 1890, becoming the first state to grant full voting rights to women. The state motto is "Equal Rights."

Q Who was the first woman to run for the U.S. presidency?

A In 1872, the Equal Rights Party nominated Victoria Claflin Woodhull for the Presidency. This was at a time when, nationwide, women were not allowed to vote.

Q Who was "Ma" Ferguson?

A The first woman Governor of Texas and second woman in
the United States to be elected Governor was Miriam
Amanda Wallace Ferguson, wife of former Governor James
E. Ferguson, who had been thrown out of office. When
James Ferguson failed to get his name on the ballot in 1924,
Miriam entered the race. Although "Ma" Ferguson was
elected on the same day as Wyoming's Nellie Ross, she was
inaugurated fifteen days later. Her nickname came from her
initials.

**Q Who became the first woman to head the government of an
Islamic nation?**

A On December 2, 1988, Benazir Bhutto was sworn in as Prime
Minister of Pakistan, becoming the first female Prime
Minister of an Islamic State.

**Q Who was the first woman to serve as Britain's Prime
Minister?**

A Margaret Thatcher, who assumed the position of Prime
Minister in May 1979, had been the Conservative Party
Leader of the Opposition since 1970. She resigned her office
in November 1990.

Q Which animal is the oldest domestic animal?

A The dog, which has been domesticated for 12,000 to 14,000 years.

Q When were cats first domesticated?

A Cats were domesticated in ancient Egypt as long as 4,000 years ago.

Q What is the world's largest reptile?

A The Saltwater or Estuarine Crocodile can grow to be more than 23 feet in length and weigh more than 3,300 pounds. The adult males are typically about 17 feet long and weigh 1,000 pounds. They are native to tropical regions of Asia and Australasia. In Australia, they are called Australian Saltwater Crocodiles; it is here that Crocodile Dundee developed his reputation by fighting these dangerous reptiles.

Q What is the largest reptile in the United States?

A The American alligator. Most male adult alligators are around ten or eleven feet long and weigh 450 to 600 pounds. They are found in swamps, marshes, rivers, and lakes in the southeastern United States, from Texas to the Carolinas.

Q How many American homes have reptiles as pets?

A As of 2000, nearly 4 million American households had a reptile as a pet. Turtles, snakes, and frogs are the most popular reptilian pets. More than 63 million U.S. households own one or more pets of any kind; dogs and cats remain the most popular.

Q What breed of dog is the most popular in the United States?

A As of 2006, the American Kennel Club says that Labrador retrievers are the number one registered dog in the U.S. The next most popular breeds are Yorkshire terriers, German shepherds, and golden retrievers.

Q What legendary German-born film director plays the chauffeur in *Sunset Boulevard* (1950)?

A Erich Von Stroheim, who directed such films as *Greed* (1924) and *The Merry Widow* (1925). Ironically, Stroheim couldn't drive.

Q What is the name of Gloria Swanson's dead boyfriend in *Sunset Boulevard*?

A Joe Gillis, played by William Holden.

Q Name the film star and director of such silent classics as *The General* and *The Navigator* who also appeared in *Sunset Boulevard* (1950)?

A Buster Keaton, who played a card-playing friend of Norma Desmond in *Sunset Boulevard.*

Q Name the two actors who have won back-to-back Oscars for Best Actor.

A Spencer Tracy won Best Actor for *Captains Courageous* in 1937 and repeated in 1938 for his role in *Boys Town.* Tom Hanks won Best Actor for *Philadelphia* in 1993 and struck gold again the following year with *Forrest Gump.*

Q Who has won back-to-back Oscars for Best Actress?

A Luise Rainer won Best Actress for *The Great Ziegfeld* in 1936 and again for *The Good Earth* the following year. Katharine Hepburn won Best Actress for *Guess Who's Coming to Dinner* in 1967 and repeated in 1968 for her role in *The Lion in Winter.*

Q Who was the author of the 1963 novel, *The Spy Who Came in From the Cold*?

A John le Carré is the nom de plume of David Cornwell, who was born in 1931 in Dorset, England. Le Carré's third novel, *The Spy Who Came in from the Cold*, was the one that secured him a worldwide reputation.

Q When was the modern game of tennis introduced to England?

A The standard belief is that Major W. C. Wingfield introduced lawn tennis at a garden party in 1873. He published the first book of rules for what he called "Sphairistiké, or Lawn Tennis" that year and took out a patent on his game in 1874. However, researchers have concluded that there were earlier versions of tennis, and that the first tennis club was established by the Englishman Harry Gem in Leamington in 1872.

Q When was the modern game of tennis introduced to the United States?

A Credit is given to Mary Outerbridge of New York for bringing a set of rackets and balls to her brother, a director of the Staten Island Cricket and Baseball Club in 1874. She had seen a tennis match in Bermuda. But, research has shown that William Appleton of Nahant, Massachusetts, may have owned the first lawn tennis set in the United States.

Q How many Wimbledon singles tournaments did Martina Navratilova win?

A Martina Navratilova won nine Wimbledon singles tournaments. Her first Wimbledon win was in 1978; she also won in 1979, 1982–1987, and again in 1990. Navratilova, the top ranked woman player from 1982–1986, also won four U.S. Open titles, three Australian Open titles, and two French Open titles.

Q When was the first tennis championship tournament held at Wimbledon?

A In 1877, the Wimbledon club decided to hold a tennis championship, and standardized the rules. They decided on a rectangular court 78 feet long by 27 feet wide, and adopted a method of scoring; these decisions remain part of the modern rules. The first winner of the All-England Championship was Spencer Gore.

Q Who was the first African-American male to win a major U.S. tennis title?

A Arthur Ashe (1943-1993) won 51 titles, including the 1968 U.S. Open, the 1970 Australian Open, and the 1975 Wimbledon title. After suffering from a heart attack and undergoing quadruple bypass surgery, Ashe retired as a player in 1980 with a professional record of 818 wins, 260 losses.

Q Who was the first African-American to win the Wimbledon tournament?

A In 1957, Althea Gibson became the first African-American woman to win at Wimbledon and Forest Hills. That same year, she was named Woman Athlete of the Year by the Associated Press. Gibson was the first African-American to play in the U.S. grass court championships at Forest Hills, N.Y. (1950), and at Wimbledon, England (1951).

Q What country is credited with starting the Christmas tree decorating tradition as we know it?

A Germany, in the sixteenth century. Early Mystery plays performed on December 24th for Adam and Eve's feast day used a decorated evergreen as a symbol of the Tree of Life in Eden (called *Paradis Baum*). The tree was decorated with apples. It caught on, and soon people were bringing their own Paradise Trees into their homes and decorating them with food.

Q What is George Eliot's real name?

A Mary Ann Evans (1819–1880) who is the author of many literary classics, including *Adam Bede, Mill on the Floss, Middlemarch*, and *Silas Marner*.

Q **Who was Deacon Brodie? What part did he play in literature?**

A Deacon Brodie was the inspiration for Robert Louis Stevenson's Dr. Jekyll and Mr. Hyde. Brodie was a pillar of Edinburgh society who lived a double life: straight-laced establishment member turned arch criminal terrifying the developing capital city of Edinburgh in the late 18th century. Nearly a century later, Stevenson told the story of the infamous Mr. Hyde.

Q **Which literary classic was chosen by the Modern Library as the number one book of the twentieth century?**

A James Joyce's *Ulysses*. The Modern Library panel adjudged the 1922 classic as the premier book of the last century.

Q **When did Aldous Huxley publish his novel *Brave New World*? When was *1984*, by George Orwell, published?**

A Huxley's view of the future was published in 1933; Orwell's story of a future society run by Big Brother and the Thought Police—*1984*—was published in 1949.

Q What is a theremin?

A It is an electronic musical instrument invented by Professor Leon Theremin. The theremin is probably best known for its spooky sounds in many old science fiction movies and in the Beach Boys' song "Good Vibrations." A musician plays the theremin by waving his hands around two electrodes, controlling the tone and loudness.

Q Where does the word "boycott" come from?

A The word "boycott" comes from Captain Charles Cunningham Boycott, who was the agent for the Earl of Erne's estates in County Mayo, Ireland. In 1880, when Boycott refused to reduce rents, the tenants shunned Boycott, and avoided any communication with him.

Q Who first discovered the moons of Jupiter?

A Galileo Galilei made the telescope famous for his astronomical observations in 1609. He was the first to provide drawings of the moons of Jupiter and document the phases of Venus.

Q Who created the library in Alexandria in the fourth century B.C.E.?

A Ptolemy I, King of Egypt

Q How long did Britain's Queen Victoria reign?

A Not for nothing was the latter half of the 19th century called the Victorian Age—Victoria was Queen of the United Kingdom of Great Britain and Ireland from 1837 until her death in 1901. Her husband was Prince Consort Albert, from Saxe-Colburg-Gotha, a German state.

Q Who is the author of the following quotes?
   "A penny saved is a penny earned."
   "Any fool can criticize, condemn and complain, and most fools do."
   "Early to bed, early to rise makes a man healthy, wealthy, and wise."
   "Fish and visitors smell in three days."
   "Never leave that till tomorrow which you can do today."

A Benjamin Franklin (1706-1790).

Q In the United Sates, there once was a state of Franklin. Where was it located?

A In August 1784, delegates from what is now eastern Tennessee gathered in Jonesborough to study the issue of seceding from North Carolina. By December, separation was a done deal. They named the new state Franklin, after Benjamin Franklin, one of America's founding fathers. Franklin's only governor was John Sevier, a war hero who had fought against the Indians. The state of Franklin disappeared forever when it was ceded to a new federal government in the late 1780s. It became known as the Southwest Territory.

Q Each of the following familiar quotes is taken from a play by William Shakespeare. From which play is each taken?
"The lady doth protest too much, methinks."
'To be or not to be: that is the question."
"Something is rotten in the state of Denmark"
"To sleep, perchance to dream."
"I must be cruel only to be kind."
"The play's the thing Wherein I'll catch the conscience of the King."

A All of them are from *Hamlet*.

Q What famous American said "You can fool all the people some of the time, and some of the people all the time, but you cannot fool all the people all the time"?

A Sixteenth President of the United States, Abraham Lincoln.

Q What famous American said, "Politics is not a bad profession. If you succeed there are many rewards, if you disgrace yourself you can always write a book"?

A Fortieth President of the United States, Ronald Reagan.

Q What did President Harry S Truman say about getting things done?

A "It is amazing what you can accomplish if you do not care who gets the credit."

Q Frank Capra, George Stevens, and William Wyler formed an independent production company that folded after making only one picture. Name the company and the movie.

A Liberty Pictures dissolved after making *It's A Wonderful Life* (1946).

Q What do we call the days in which the Sun's path is farthest from the equator?

A The summer and winter solstices, which fall on June 21 or 22 and December 21 or 22 of each year. The solstices are either of the two moments in the year when the Sun's path is farthest north or south from the equator. In the Northern Hemisphere, the summer solstice is the longest day of the year, measured by the amount of daylight, and the winter solstice is the shortest day.

Q How many medals did Jim Thorpe win at the 1912 Stockholm Olympic games?

A In 1912, Native American James "Jim" Thorpe won the decathlon and the pentathlon by wide margins at the Olympic Games in Stockholm. But, the Amateur Athletic Union stripped him of his gold medals after they discovered that he had been paid to play semiprofessional baseball in 1909. Years after Thorpe's death in 1953, his amateur status was restored, and his Olympic gold medals were given to his family in 1983.

Q Who is the only player in NBA history to score 100 points in a game?

A Wilt Chamberlain. The center for the Philadelphia Warriors scored 100 points on March 2, 1962 against the New York Knicks. The Warriors won, 169-147.

Q In what year did Pocahontas marry John Rolfe?

A Pocahontas is the nickname of Matoaka (1595–1617), a Native American who converted to Christianity and was baptized Rebecca. She married Englishman John Rolfe in 1614. In 1616, she and her husband sailed to England, where she was presented to the court of James I. Before she could return to America, she contracted smallpox and died.

Q What is the well-known story about Pocahontas taught to every American student?

A Pocahontas is immortalized in American history because of the often-told story about her plea to save the life of Jamestown's military leader, Captain John Smith. In December 1607, Smith had been taken prisoner, and was about to be clubbed to death by the local Native Americans, led by Pocahontas' father. The story eventually became embellished into the tale of Pocahontas bravely flinging herself across his body just before the club came down, declaring that he must spared, and that she would rather be killed first.

Q How long have people cooked with chili peppers?

A Archaeologists have found evidence in southwestern Ecuador that chilies were cultivated and used in cooking 6,000 years ago.

Q Who invented the assembly line?

A Automobile manufacturer Ransom E. Olds introduced the moving assembly line in 1901. Henry Ford, who is often credited with inventing the assembly line, improved the assembly line by installing conveyer belts, which speeded up the process considerably.

Q Who invented the radio?

A Guglielmo Marconi (1874–1937) was an Italian physicist and inventor of a successful system of radiotelegraphy (1895). He later worked on the development of short-wave wireless communication, which constitutes the basis of nearly all modern long-distance radio. Marconi shared the Nobel Prize in physics in 1909.

Q Who invented vulcanized rubber?

A Charles Goodyear discovered that, by mixing the crude rubber with sulfur and heating the mixture for a long time, rubber was transformed into the elastic material we know today. He named the process vulcanizing.

Q Who invented the lighter-than-air vehicle named the zeppelin?

A Count Ferdinand Graf von Zeppelin (1838–1917) was the German military officer who developed the rigid dirigible that became known as the zeppelin. The airship's first trial was in July 1900. Although zeppelins had some popularity, and passengers made many trips without accidents or loss of life, they are perhaps best remembered because of the tragic explosion of the *Hindenburg* on May 6, 1937, in Lakehurst, New Jersey. Thirty-six people died.

Q Who invented the windshield wiper?

A Mary Anderson was granted her first patent for a window-cleaning device in November 1903. Her invention could clean snow, rain, or sleet from a windshield by using a handle inside the car. Windshield wipers were standard equipment on all American cars by 1916.

Q Did Stephen Crane, author of the well-known Civil War novel, *The Red Badge of Courage*, serve in the War Between the States?

A No, Crane was born in 1871, after the war was over.

Q Who was the first scientist to discover the many uses of peanuts, including peanut butter?

A Born a slave in Mississippi, George Washington Carver (1864–1943) developed several hundred uses for peanuts, sweet potatoes, and soybeans, and developed a new type of cotton known as Carver's hybrid. Carver dedicated his life to bettering the position of African-Americans and improving the economic prospects of the South.

Q Who invented the safety pin?

A The safety pin was invented by Walter Hunt of New York while he was absent-mindedly twisting a piece of wire. On April 10, 1849, Hunt patented the safety pin, but he later sold the patent for a few hundred dollars. His invention made babies very grateful.

Q Who invented the motorcycle?

A In 1867, Sylvester Howard Roper of Roxbury, Massachusetts had built a steam-powered motorcycle. But, German inventor Gottlieb Daimler is credited with building the first modern motorcycle in 1885, which was powered by a single-cylinder gas-powered engine. Daimler later teamed up with Karl Benz, forming the Daimler-Benz Corporation, to make automobiles.

Q What French aristocrat helped the American colonists out during the American Revolution?

A Marquis de Lafayette (1757–1834) was a French aristocrat who offered his services, and fought with the American colonists against the British in the American Revolution. Given a commission as a major general by the colonists, Lafayette fought with distinction, particularly at the Battle of Brandywine, Pennsylvania, in 1777. After the war, he returned to France; on visits to the new United States of America, he was treated like a hero.

Q What French pirate helped out the Americans during the War of 1812?

A Jean Lafitte, a privateer and smuggler, interrupted his pirating activities to join the fight for the United States against the British at the Battle of New Orleans (December 1814–January 1815). For his help, Andrew Jackson personally commended Laffite, and President James Madison issued a pardon for Lafitte and his men.

Q Who played this French pirate in the 1958 film, *The Buccaneer*?

A Dark-haired Yul Brynner was Jean Lafitte in the 1958 remake of a 1938 film. Frederic March played Lafitte in the 1938 film.

Q Which scientist was the first to suggest that the earth traveled around the Sun, rather than the other way around?

A Nicolaus Copernicus (1473–1543) was a Polish astronomer who proposed that the Earth is a planet that orbits the Sun annually. This representation of the heavens is called the heliocentric, or "Sun-centered" view of the planets.

Q Who invented basketball?

A In 1891, trying to create an indoor athletic activity for male students at the School for Christian Workers in Springfield, Massachusetts, James Naismith developed basketball and its original thirteen rules.

Q When was volleyball invented?

A Not far from Springfield, in the city of Holyoke, Massachusetts, in 1895, William Morgan, a YMCA instructor, created the game of volleyball, which he called *mintonette*. Morgan borrowed elements from both tennis and handball. In 1900, a special ball was designed for the sport.

Q Rank these international cities by amount of average annual rainfall: San Francisco, New York, London, Dublin.

A New York has by far the most rain. Average annual precipitation, ranked by wettest to driest: New York—46.7 inches, London—29.7 inches, Dublin—29.2 inches, San Francisco—20.4 inches.

Q In a 2006 survey by *Reader's Digest*, which city did reporters find to be the "politest city" of the 36 cities? Which city was described as the "rudest city"?

A Believe it or not, New York City was considered to be the most polite, beating out cities such as London, Toronto, and Zurich. The reporters observed whether people held doors, said "thank you," and were helpful to strangers.
Although they dispute the findings, Mumbai, India was ranked last—the rudest city.

Q Why are London police officers called "bobbies"?

A When Sir Robert Peel introduced his Act for Policing the Metropolis in 1829, the members of the Metropolitan Police (London's first police force) were nicknamed Bobbies after Sir Robert.

Q Who was the youngest man to become president?

A Theodore Roosevelt was 42 when he assumed the presidency in 1901.

Q Who was the youngest man to be elected president?

A John F. Kennedy was only 43 when he was elected president in 1960.

Q Who was the oldest sitting president?

A When he left office in 1989, Ronald Reagan was 77 years old.

Q Who was Dick Turpin? When did he live?

A Dick Turpin was born in rural Essex, England, in 1706. Legend has transformed Dick Turpin into a swashbuckling, devil-may-care character, but the real Turpin may have been less than that. He was hanged as a highwayman in 1739.

Q Who was Englebert Humperdink?

A Humperdink (1854–1921) was a German composer, whose best-known opera is *Hansel & Gretel*. Englebert Humperdink is also the name that Arnold Dorsey adopted in his pop music career, singing such songs as "Please Release Me."

Q What is the name of the doomed boat on *Gilligan's Island* (1964–1967)?

A *The S. S. Minnow.*

Q What were the station call letters where Mary Tyler Moore worked on *The Mary Tyler Moore Show* (1970-1977)?

A WJM.

Q In the last episode of *The Mary Tyler Moore Show*, all the characters, save one, are fired from the station. Which character manages to keep their job?

A The bumbling anchorman, Ted Baxter, is the only one to keep his job.

Q How would you define "agoraphobia"?

A The simple answer is that agoraphobia is an anxiety disorder—an intense and irrational fear of being in places or situations from which escape might be difficult and where one would be helpless. People who suffer from agoraphobia fear crowds in public or confined spaces. In Greek, it means "fear of the marketplace."

Q Is "dendrophobia" the fear of dentists?

A Dendrophobia is an intense, overpowering fear of trees. Dentophobia is an intense fear of dentists.

Q Who was the first African-American to have his own television show?

A Nat "King" Cole was the first African-American to have both his own radio show, and later, his own television show. Cole's radio show, which lasted for four years, began in 1946. In October 1956, Nat hosted his own TV show on NBC.

Q What newspaper gossip columnist ended up hosting one of the most popular musical variety television shows of all time?

A Ed Sullivan, who was a Broadway columnist with the New York *Daily News,* hosted a musical variety show every Sunday night for more than two decades (1948–1971). Sullivan had his own unique diction and hand gestures, supplying comics with loads of material.

Q What television show made Dick Clark nationally famous?

A Dick Clark was the host of *American Bandstand*, the first network television show devoted to rock and roll. This Philadelphia-based afternoon show had its ABC debut on August 5, 1957.

Q When was the first commercial color television broadcast?

A On June 25, 1951, CBS broadcast a one-hour special from New York to four American cities.

Q **Who was the host of the *Today* show when it debuted on NBC in 1952?**

A Dave Garroway was the host from 1952 to 1961. John Chancellor had a stint in 1961 and 1962, and Hugh Downs took over in 1962, running to 1971.

Q **Which future Academy Award winning actress was a "Today Girl" in 1953?**

A Years before Estelle Parsons won the 1967 Academy Award for Best Supporting Actress for her performance in *Bonnie and Clyde*, Estelle Parsons was on the Today Show.

Q **In a 2006 article, who did the magazine *Entertainment Weekly* name as the greatest sidekick of all time?**

A Ed McMahon, of course. Rounding out the top five: Robin (Batman's ward), Seinfeld's George Costanza, Han Solo's co-pilot Chewbacca, and Ethel Mertz of *I Love Lucy* fame.

Q **What is the name of the newspaper where Peter Parker gets a job in *Spider-Man* (2002)?**

A *The Daily Bugle.*

Q When did Coca-Cola® introduce "New Coke"?

A In 1985, Coca-Cola decided to change the ninety-nine year formula of Coke, and introduced "New Coke." After the public outcry, they brought back a version of the original formula.

Q What was the name of the Ramones's first album? What were the first names of the members of the band?

A Their 1976 debut album was called *The Ramones*. All of the Ramones took the surname Ramone; at the time of their first record, the first names of the band were Joey, Johnny, Dee Dee, and Tommy. Many consider the Ramones to be the world's first punk band.

Q Why should you be concerned if your elderly grandparent suddenly likes rock and roll?

A According to a recent report by researchers at Italy's National Center for Research and Care of Alzheimer's Disease, sudden changes in musical taste may be an indication that an elderly person is suffering from dementia.

Q Does your body temperature stay the same throughout the day?

A Typically, a person's body temperature rises during the late afternoon and drops late at night.

Q Why is Edith Head famous?

A Edith Head (1897-1981) was a dress designer who became the premier costume designer in Hollywood. Her first film was *She Done Him Wrong* (1933) with Mae West. During her career, she was nominated for 34 Academy Awards and won a total of eight awards, She won Oscars for *The Heiress, Samson and Delilah* (both 1949), *All About Eve, A Place in the Sun* (1951), *Roman Holiday* (1953), *Sabrina* (1954), *The Facts of Life* (1960), and *The Sting* (1973).

Q When did Americans start drinking tea?

A Governor Peter Stuyvesant brought the first tea to the Dutch settlement of New Amsterdam around 1650. Settlers there quickly adopted the new beverage. In fact, when the English arrived, they found that the small settlement, which they re-named New York, consumed more tea at that time then all of England.

Q How did "Molly Pitcher" earn her nickname and her fame?

A Some don't believe that Molly Pitcher ever really existed. Of those that do, most say that Mary Ludwig Hays McCauley was Molly Pitcher. She gained her fame by putting down her water pitcher to join the fight at the June 1778 Battle of Monmouth. After her artilleryman husband was wounded, Molly grabbed the rammer staff and began to fire the cannon at the British.

Q When was the submarine first used in combat?

A In 1776, American David Bushnell built a human-powered, one-man submarine named the *Turtle*. It was able to dive and surface, and he made three unsuccessful attempts to sink British warships and break the British blockade of New York harbor.

Q How much of the earth's surface is covered with ice?

A About ten per cent of the earth's surface is covered with ice. The icy cover has ranged from about 10 percent to around 30 percent during the last Ice Age.

Q **When was the Coronation of Great Britain's Queen Elizabeth II?**

A Elizabeth the Second, Queen of the United Kingdom of Great Britain and Northern Ireland and Her other Realms and Territories, Head of the Commonwealth, Defender of the Faith, was crowned on June 2, 1953 at London's Westminster Abbey. However, she had ascended to the British throne previously, on February 6, 1952, after the death of her father, King George VI.

Q **What elements are the main components of air on earth?**

A Air is primarily composed of nitrogen and oxygen.

Q **What place is the oldest permanent European settlement in what is now the United States?**

A The French established a fort and colony on the St. Johns River in 1564, but St. Augustine, Florida, founded by Spaniard Pedro Menendez in 1565, is the oldest permanent European settlement in the U.S. St. Augustine was established forty-two years before the English colony at Jamestown, Virginia.

Q Who was the author of the pamphlet *Common Sense*?

A Thomas Paine formulated his ideas on American independence form England in Common Sense, published in January 1776.

Q Who attended the Boston Tea Party on December 16, 1763?

A Angered by the fact that the tariff on tea had been eliminated in England, but was still in effect in the colonies, locals, in Indian disguise, protested by dumping the tea from three ships into Boston harbor.

Q "These are the times that try men's souls." What American patriot authored this sentence?

A Thomas Paine, *The American Crisis*. Paine wrote sixteen influential papers, published between 1776 and 1783.

Q Who was John Hancock? On what famous American document did he put his "John Hancock" signature?

A A. John Hancock was a prominent Boston merchant; he was the President of the Continental Congress and the first signer of the Declaration of Independence.

Q What is the name of the first American patriot to die in what was called "the Boston Massacre" on March 5, 1770?

A The first American to die in what was the beginning of the American Revolution was Crispus Attucks, a free black man.

Q Which forces were victorious at the Battle of Saratoga (1777)?

A Considered the major turning point of the American Revolution, the Battle of Saratoga showed the world that the American army was capable of defeating the British. After this American victory, European powers, particularly the French, began to support the American cause.

Q Which forces were victorious at the Battle of Yorktown (1781)?

A The American colonial forces. British General Lord Charles Cornwallis surrendered to General George Washington. The Battle of Yorktown is considered to be the final battle of the American Revolution.

Q How long can giraffes go without drinking water?

A Giraffes can go for two weeks without water, relying on the water content of their food.

Q Who were the authors of the *Federalist Papers*?

A *The Federalist* is a series of 85 essays written by Alexander Hamilton, John Jay, and James Madison between October 1787 and May 1788. The essays were published anonymously, under the pen name "Publius."

Q How long did the United States live under the Articles of Confederation?

A From March 1, 1781, until March 4, 1789, when the Constitution was declared to be in effect.

Q What name is given to the first ten amendments to the Constitution?

A The first ten amendments are known as the Bill of Rights. These amendments guarantee such basic American freedoms as freedom of speech, religion, etc.

Q Which American car is named after the founder of the city of Detroit?

A The Cadillac was named after eighteenth century French explorer Antoine de la Mothe, sieur de Cadillac, the founder of the city of Detroit.

Q Who was the first president of the United States?

A In 1781, under the Articles of Confederation, Congress elected John Hanson of Maryland as the first president. The first president under the new system of government established by the Constitution, was, of course, George Washington.

Q When was George Washington, who became known as the "Father of our Country," born? When did he die?

A Born in 1732 into a Virginia planter family, George Washington served his country until he died of a throat infection on December 14, 1799.

Q What political party did Washington belong to?

A None. Washington was chosen to be president before the development of political parties.

Q Who killed Alexander Hamilton?

A On July 11,1804, Vice President Aaron Burr shot former Secretary of the Treasury Alexander Hamilton in a duel in Weehawken, New Jersey. Hamilton died the next day.

Q **What popular object found in almost every American home purportedly includes numerous Masonic symbols?**

A The dollar bill. The dollar bill's reverse side contains what many believe to be Masonic symbolism, such as the eye in the triangle above the unfinished pyramid.

Q **Which person gave the "Ain't I a Woman?" speech at the 1851 Women's Rights Convention in Akron, Ohio?**

A Sojourner Truth (1797–1883), who was a freed slave, dedicated her life to preaching to all about the abolition of slavery and the cause of women's rights.

Q **Who was the most famous "conductor" of the Underground Railroad?**

A Harriet Tubman, who escaped from slavery in 1849, made nineteen trips back to the South and helped deliver hundreds of slaves to freedom. She had to elude capture by bounty hunters, as there was a $40,000 bounty for her capture.

Q Although making up only one percent of the population of the North, African-Americans made up what percentage of the Union Army at the end of the Civil War?

A By the end of the Civil War, ten percent of the Union Army were black soldiers. Many of them were freed slaves from the Border States.

Q Who were "the Buffalo Soldiers"?

A After the Civil War, the U.S. created fighting units of African-American soldiers. They played an important role in the history of the American West. In addition to combat duties, the buffalo soldiers explored and mapped much of the Southwest, strung telegraph lines, built frontier outposts, and protected settlers from attacks. The Cheyenne named them the "buffalo soldiers."

Q Who fought at the Battle of Wounded Knee (December 29, 1890)?

A The Battle of Wounded Knee was the last significant conflict fought between Native Americans and the victorious U. S. troops. Over 200 Sioux, led by chief Big Foot, were massacred at Wounded Knee Creek, South Dakota, by U.S. 7th Cavalry.

Q When was the first Model T built?

A Henry Ford first marketed the Model T in October, 1908. Nicknamed the "Tin Lizzie," the car dominated American car sales for eighteen years.

Q What was the Manhattan Project?

A The Manhattan Project involved the research and the development of the atomic bomb during WW2. With the belief that Germany might successfully develop an atomic bomb, a group of physicists, including Albert Einstein, approached President Roosevelt about establishing an atomic bomb research program.

Q What future American president was the Allied Supreme Commander in World War II?

A Thirty-fourth president Dwight D. Eisenhower was the Allied Supreme Commander.

Q How many presidents were never married?

A Only one—fifteenth president of the United States, James Buchanan.

Q One American general made a famous vow "I shall return" in 1942; who was he and where was he promising to return?

A The Philippine Islands. When General Douglas MacArthur was forced off the islands by the Japanese in 1942, he said "I shall return." In 1944, MacArthur did return to the Philippines to defeat the Japanese.

Q Which future president was the skipper of the PT109 during the Second World War?

A John F. Kennedy, a junior officer and hero in the Navy. When asked about his heroism, Kennedy said, "It was involuntary. They sank my boat."

Q Which future president was the youngest U.S. Navy fighter pilot in WWII?

A After becoming, at nineteen, the youngest Navy fighter pilot, George H. W. Bush flew fifty-eight WWII missions.

Q How did Douglas "Wrong Way" Corrigan get his nickname?

A On July 17, 1938, Douglas Corrigan filed a flight plan at Floyd Bennett Field in New York to fly to California, but ended up in Dublin 29 hours later.

Q What archaeological site was recently discovered to be the oldest known city in the Americas?

A Researchers investigating an archaeological site known as Caral, 120 miles north of Lima, Peru, in the Supe River Valley, have concluded that it dates back to before 2700 B.C.E. This makes it 1,500 years older than scientists had previously thought urban civilization existed in the New World. Much more archaeological work needs to be done.

Q Who were the Aztecs? Where did they live?

A The Aztecs were Native Americans who lived in central Mexico at the time of the Spanish conquest. The arrival of the conquistador Cortes in 1519 heralded the collapse of their empire. They are known for their advanced architecture, mathematics, and art.

Q Who were the Mayans? Where did they live?

A The Mayans were Amerindians who inhabited central America, in what is now the Yucatan peninsula, Guatemala, El Salvador, and Honduras. The Mayans, who were pyramid-builders, thrived in the years of 300 to 900 A.D.

Q   Where did the Incas live?

A   The Inca civilization was centered at Cuzco, Peru. At the time of Spanish conquest in 1532, the Incas dominated the Andean area, with an empire containing sixteen million people and extending some 3,000 miles, including parts of Ecuador, Chile, Bolivia, and Argentina.

Q   When did the Vikings colonize Greenland and explore North America?

A   Eric the Red established the first European settlement on Greenland in about 985 A.D., after he was exiled from Iceland. Eric the Red's son, Leif Eriksson, is thought to have been among the first Europeans to set foot on North American soil around 1000 A.D. In 1963, archaeologists found ruins of a Viking-type settlement at L'Anse aux Meadows, in northern Newfoundland.

Q   When was the first English colony founded in Newfoundland?

A   Sailing for England, Italian explorer John Cabot sighted Newfoundland in 1497, and Sir Humphrey Gilbert claimed Newfoundland for Britain in 1583. Lured by the great fishing on the Grand Banks, John Guy, an English merchant, brought 39 settlers to Conception Bay in 1610.

Q Where can you find the Blow Me Down Mountains?

A In the Blow Me Down Provincial Park in western Newfoundland, situated on a peninsula between Lark and York Harbors. These mountains also go by the name of the Blomidon Mountains.

Q Do any mammals fly?

A Yes, bats fly. Other mammals are superlative leapers and gliders, but only bats can actually fly.

Q The raccoon, a nocturnal mammal, is known for its distinctive black facial mask and four-to-six alternating black and brown bands on its furry tail. What do raccoons like to eat?

A Although they enjoy busting into campsites, breaking into houses, and knocking over garbage cans, devouring everything in sight, their supposed favorite food is small fish. Raccoons are omnivorous mammals whose diet may include grapes, nuts, insects, mice, small mammals, larvae, eggs, fish, frogs, and acorns—in other words, they eat almost anything.

Q Which president of the United States had a pet raccoon he named Rebecca?

A Thirtieth president of the United States Calvin Coolidge kept a raccoon as a pet. The raccoon was sent by some Mississippians for eating, but "Silent Cal" decided to keep it as a pet. Coolidge also made White House pets of a bear, a donkey, a bobcat, a lion, and a hippo.

Q When were the first presidential candidate debates?

A In September and October of 1960, Senator John F. Kennedy and Vice President Richard Nixon debated four times.

Q How many presidents were Roman Catholic?

A One. John F. Kennedy, 35th President, who was elected in 1960.

Q On the Fourth of July, 1826, the United States had its fiftieth birthday. What else made that day memorable?

A Former presidents John Adams and Thomas Jefferson both died that day. Five years later on Independence Day, James Monroe died.

Q **What are the two main types of clouds?**

A All clouds are visible collections of water or ice suspended in the atmosphere. The two general types of clouds are cumulus and stratus. Cumulus "heaped" clouds, which are rounded on top and may be very tall, are the result of convection in unstable air. Stratus "layered" clouds are generally flat and horizontally layered. Clouds are also named according to their elevation and whether precipitation is falling. Stratus clouds at high levels, over 20,000 feet above the earth, are called cirrus clouds; nimbus clouds are generally dark, with falling precipitation.

Q **Who made the discovery that clouds could be seeded, causing it to rain?**

A Dr. Vincent J. Schaefer, the father of modern weather modification, conducted the first field experiments in 1946 at the General Electric Laboratory in Schenectady, New York, altering the physical processes that lead to the formation and coagulation of water droplets and ice crystals in clouds. Schaefer discovered that clouds could be seeded with dry ice or salt crystals in order to encourage the condensation of water droplets needed for rain or snow.

Q What is "brain freeze"? What happens when you are eating ice cream and you get an intense pain in the forehead?

A The "brain freeze" reaction, often called "ice cream headaches," can be triggered after a very cold substance, such as ice cream, comes into contact with the roof of the mouth. This irritates nerves in the region, which causes the blood vessels in the brain to dilate. The headache usually lasts ten to twenty seconds. The pain may be avoided in the first place by consuming the cold food or beverage more slowly. Some people are more susceptible than others—it has been estimated that 30% of the population experiences a more intense brain freeze.

Q What is the name of Barbra Streisand's first movie role?

A *Funny Girl* (1968), in which Barbra played Fannie Brice, was a movie made of the earlier hit Broadway musical. In the film, Omar Sharif played her husband, Nick Arnstein. It was directed by William Wyler.

"People (who need people)" was the biggest hit song to come out of the show.

Q In how many films did Basil Rathbone star as Sherlock Holmes?

A Fourteen films and hundreds of radio broadcasts.

Q What was the title of Stevie Wonder's first hit, released by Motown when he was only twelve years old?

A "Fingertips, Part 2," which hit the Number One spot in August, 1963. In those days, he was known as Little Stevie Wonder.

Q In what year did the Beatles lead the British Invasion of America?

A The Beatles first appeared on *The Ed Sullivan Show* on February 9, 1964. They performed "All My Loving," "'Til There was You," "She Loves You," "I Saw Her Standing There," and "I Want to Hold Your Hand." Over 70 million Americans watched the show.

Q What show starred David Janssen as Dr. Richard Kimble?

A *The Fugitive* (1963–1967) was the series whose lead character is a doctor who has been convicted of murdering his wife, and is now on the run, searching for the one-armed man he saw running from his house the night of the murder.

Q   What private eye show starred David Janssen? Who played his secretary Sam, whose face we never see?

A   *Richard Diamond, Private Detective* (1957–1960). Mary Tyler Moore played Sam, who speaks to Diamond on the phone, but her face is never shown.

Q   When did Muhammad Ali first capture the world heavyweight crown?

A   Muhammad Ali, then known as Cassius Clay, defeated Sonny Liston in seven rounds on February 25, 1964, in Miami Beach, Florida.

Q   Who won the "fight of the century" fought between Muhammad Ali and Joe Frazier at Madison Square Garden on March 8, 1971?

A   Muhammad Ali lost the heavyweight title to Joe Frazier in a unanimous decision after being knocked down in the 15th round. Ali regained his title by defeating Frazier in a rematch in 1974.

Q In which different weight classes did Ray Leonard win the championship during his illustrious boxing career?

A In addition to winning the gold medal at the 1976 Olympics, Ray Leonard held championships in five different weight classes: Welterweight (1979). Jr. Middleweight (1981), Middleweight (1987), Super Middleweight (1988), and Light Heavyweight (1988).

Q Name the actors who played the "Bad" and the "Ugly" in the 1966 film *The Good, The Bad and The Ugly*.

A The "Bad" was played by Lee Van Cleef and the "Ugly" by Eli Wallach. The "Good" was, of course, played by Clint Eastwood.

Q Where did the swimsuit called the bikini get its name?

A Two-piece bathing suits for women already existed, but in 1946 Louis Reard, a French engineer running his mother's lingerie business, came up with a new swimsuit design known as "le bikini." The new design debuted shortly after U.S. nuclear tests on the Bikini Atoll in the South Pacific, and Reard thought such a name would help the commercial success of his "explosive" design.

Q What is the rule for plot technique in novels that is known as "Chekhov's dictum"?

A If you say in the first chapter that there is a rifle hanging on the wall, in the second or third chapter it absolutely must go off. If it's not going to be fired, it shouldn't be hanging there.
—Anton Chekhov (1860-1904)

Q What does the Latin phrase "quid pro quo" mean?

A "Something for something." Quid pro quo is an exchange—something given or received in return for something else.

Q How far away is the Andromeda Galaxy?

A The Andromeda Galaxy is 2.2 million light-years away from Earth.

Q What star is known as the "Dog Star"?

A The "Dog Star," the brightest star in the night sky, is Sirius, Alpha Canis Majoris. It is twenty times more luminous than Earth's Sun, and is 8.6 light years from Earth. Some ancient cultures worshipped Sirius, including the ancient Egyptians, who constructed their temples so that light from the star could penetrate to their inner altars.

Q **What is the name of the closest star?**

A Excluding the Sun, Proxima Centauri, which is only 4.22 light years away (over 24 million miles), is the star closest to the earth. Alpha Centauri is just a hop, skip, and jump further, at 4.35 light years.

Q **What are the twelve signs of the Zodiac?**

A Aries (March 21–April 19); Taurus (April 20–May 20); Gemini (May 21–June 21); Cancer (June 22–July 22); Leo (July 23–August 22); Virgo (August 23–September 22); Libra (September 23–October 23); Scorpio (October 24–November 21); Sagittarius (November 22–December 21); Capricorn (December 22–January 19); Aquarius (January 20–February 18); Pisces (February 19–March 20).

Q **How many horns does a rhinoceroses have?**

A There are actually five different kinds of rhinoceroses: the African white, the African black, and the Sumatran rhinoceroses, all of whom have two horns; the Indian and the Javan rhinoceroses both have only one horn.

Q How fast can a rhinoceroses run?

A A rhino can charge at speeds of up to 30 miles per hour. The cornered rhino attacks with its horn.

Q Match these superheroes with their everyday names:

1. Superman	a. Dr. Bruce Banner
2. Spiderman	b. Diana Prince
3. Captain Marvel	c. Billy Batson
4. Batman	d. Peter Parker
5. Incredible Hulk	e. Clark Kent
6. Wonder Woman	f. Bruce Wayne

A 1. Superman – e. Clark Kent; 2. Spiderman – d. Peter Parker; 3. Captain Marvel – c. Billy Batson; 4. Batman – f. Bruce Wayne; 5. The Incredible Hulk – a. Dr. Bruce Banner; 6. Wonder Woman – b. Diana Prince.

Q Which multinational corporation derives its name from a Buddhist goddess of mercy?

A Canon. The name "Canon" is derived from "Kwanon." "Canon" stands for "criterion or standard of judgment." Starting out as a company with a handful of employees, Canon soon became a renowned camera maker and is now a global multimedia corporation.

Q When was the first Harley-Davidson motorcycle made?

A William S. Harley and Arthur Davidson, both in their early twenties, produced the first Harley-Davidson motorcycles in Milwaukee in 1903. The factory in which they worked was a wooden shed with the words "Harley-Davidson Motor Company" scrawled on the door.

Q How old is the Indian Motorcycle Company?

A George Hendee and Oscar Hedstrom founded the Indian Motorcycle Company in Springfield, Massachusetts, in 1901, predating Harley Davidson by two years. The company went out of business in 1953, but the name returned in 1999. Indian Motorcycles are now made in Gilroy, California, a town that calls itself the "garlic capital of the world."

Q In what year did the English settle Jamestown, Virginia?

A In 1607, the first permanent English settlement in North America was founded in Jamestown, Virginia. Jamestown was named for King James I.

Q How was Bermuda discovered?

A In 1609, while attempting to go to Jamestown, Virginia, English settlers were shipwrecked off Bermuda. Upon arrival, they claimed the island as a colony for England. Scholars believe that Shakespeare used this story as his source material for *The Tempest* (1611).

Q Who was the founder of the sect called the Shakers?

A Mother Ann Lee is generally regarded as the founder of the Shakers, who received the nickname "Shaking Quakers" because of their religious dancing. In 1774, Lee and her little group moved to America, where they lived celibate lives in rural communes, their survival assured only by converts. Today, they are probably best remembered for their spare, well-crafted wooden furniture.

Q When was the Biedermeier style of furniture introduced? How did it get its name?

A Biedermeier furniture, which has been described as utilitarian furniture for the bourgeoisie, was popular in Germany from 1810 to 1850. There was a magazine satirical character called "Papa Biedermeier," and the name was disparagingly applied to this new style for being hopelessly bourgeoisie.

Q What film was the first mass release "scratch-and-sniff" movie?

A John Waters introduced the innovative "Odorama" in the film *Polyester* (1981), which starred Divine as a suburban housewife. Heartthrob Tab Hunter was in the supporting cast.

Q *The Godfather* won the Best Picture Oscar in 1972. Did *The Godfather II* win the Academy Award for Best Picture?

A Yes, in 1974, *Godfather II* won the Best Picture Oscar.

Q What was the only X-rated film to win the Academy Award for Best Picture?

A 1969's *Midnight Cowboy* is the only X-rated film to win Best Picture Oscar; it was later edited for a R rating. The film, which starred Dustin Hoffman and Jon Voight, also won John Schlesinger the Oscar for Best Director, and Best Screenplay for Waldo Salt.

Q Which South American country is the largest, in terms of land area?

A Brazil, which has 3,286,469 square miles, occupies nearly half of the continent.

Q **Where is the longest mountain range in the world?**

A The world's longest mountain range, the Andes mountain system, stretches over 5,000 miles through seven South American countries: Argentina, Chile, Bolivia, Peru, Ecuador, Colombia, and Venezuela. The Falkland Islands and a part of Antarctica are actually continuations of the Andes.

Q **What nation of South America has the largest population?**

A The Federative Republic of Brazil, with an estimated population of over 188 million people, as of 2006.

Q **Match the South American capital cities with their countries.**

1. Argentina	a. Caracas
2. Peru	b. Santiago
3. Chile	c. Lima
4. Venezuela	d. Bogota
5. Colombia	e. Buenos Aires

A 1. Argentina – e. Buenos Aires; 2. Peru – c. Lima; 3. Chile – b. Santiago; 4. Venezuela –a. Caracas; 5. Colombia – d. Bogota.

Q When was Juan Peron the president of Argentina?

A General Juan Domingo Peron was elected president in 1946; in 1955, Peron was overthrown in a military coup, and he fled to Spain. In 1973 Juan Peron returned to Argentina after eighteen years of exile to begin a third term as president. He died in 1974. Peron's second wife, Eva, was the First lady of Argentina from 1946 until she died from cancer in 1952. Known as "Evita," she has been the subject of books, musicals, and films.

Q What 2002 study has linked people's tastes in books with the kind of dreams they have?

A Researchers from the University of Wales in Swansea have recently studied 10,000 responses from library goers and found that adults who read fiction had stranger dreams than readers of non-fiction. They also learned that fantasy readers have the most nightmares, and romance readers have dreams with great emotional intensity. This was the first major study of the relationship between the choice of reading material and the content of dreams.

Q How many of Emily Dickinson's poems were published in her lifetime?

A Seven. During her lifetime, Dickinson (1830-1886) wrote nearly eighteen hundred poems.

Q Who was Randolph Caldecott?

A Randolph Caldecott (1846–1886) was a British painter and illustrator of children's books. Since 1938, the American Library Association has given the Caldecott Medal to the illustrator of the best U.S. children's picture book of the year.

Q Who was John Newberry?

A John Newberry (1713–1767) was an English bookseller and publisher who was the first publisher of books for children. Since 1921, the American Library Association has given an annual Newberry Award to the most distinguished children's book of the year.

Q On *The Andy Griffith Show* (1960–1968), what was the name of Gomer Pyle's brother? What actors played Gomer and his brother?

A Goober, played by George Lindsey, was a character on *The Andy Griffith Show* after Jim Nabors, playing his brother Gomer Pyle, left the show to star in his own spin-off, *Gomer Pyle, U.S.M.C.*, in 1964. *The Andy Griffith Show* was set in the town of Mayberry, North Carolina.

Q Where did Matt Groening, the creator of *The Simpsons*, get the names for his TV family?

A Groening named them after his own relatives: Groening's father is named Homer, his mother is Marge, and he has two sisters, Lisa and Maggie. Bart, however, is an anagram of "brat."

Q What is the name of the 1958 film starring Andy Griffith in a role of a simple-minded hillbilly who has been drafted into the Air Force?

A *No Time for Sergeants*, which had earlier been a Broadway play, was directed by Mervyn LeRoy. Griffith played Will Stockdale; also appearing in the movie were Nick Adams and Don Knotts. Both the play and movie were based on the novel *No Time For Sergeants* by Mac Hyman, first published in 1954.

Q What was the name of Wally Cleaver's best friend in *Leave It to Beaver* (1957–1963)?

A Eddie Haskell, known best for his obsequious attitude toward persons of authority, was the best friend of Wally, Beaver's older brother.

Q What are the first names of the members of the following TV families:

The Cleavers? The Partridge Family? The Huxtables? The Simpsons?

A The Cleavers: Ward, June, Wally, and Theodore (Beaver).
The Partridges: Shirley, Keith, Laurie, Danny, Christopher, and Tracy.
The Huxtables: Heathcliff (Cliff), Clair, Theodore (Theo), Denise, Sondra, Vanessa, Rudy, and (later) Olivia.
The Simpsons: Homer, Marge, Bart, Lisa, and baby Maggie.

Q What kind of work did Wally and Beaver's dad do?

A Ward Cleaver wore a suit, went to an office in town (sometimes he even went to work on Saturday), and had a secretary. The family seemed to have a comfortable middle-class lifestyle—but, we never found out what Ward did for a living.

Q Sam Cooke had many hit records in the 1950s and '60s, including "You Send Me," "A Change is Gonna Come," and "Twistin' the Night Away." Before becoming famous as a pop singer, Sam Cooke was a member of what popular gospel group?

A Between 1951 and 1956, Sam Cooke was the lead singer of The Soul Stirrers.

Q Under what name did Ronnie Hawkins' back-up band, the Hawks, become famous?

A The Band. After playing with Hawkins, they became a back-up band for Bob Dylan. In 1966, The Band released their first album, *Music from the Big Pink.*

Q In what year and at what place was the first Woodstock Festival?

A August 15, 16, and 17, 1969, in Bethel, New York. Approximately 400,000 festival goers showed up.

Q Who was the inventor of the slot machine?

A Although there were already some mechanical poker machines around, Bavarian immigrant Charles A. Fey created the first Liberty Bell slot machine in his basement in San Francisco in 1899. The top winning combination was three bells in a row.

Q We all know Trigger was the name of Roy Rogers' horse, but what was the name of Gene Autry's horse?

A Champion.

Q What three popular recording stars were killed in a plane crash on February 3, 1959, after performing in Clear Lake, Iowa?

A Buddy Holly, Ritchie Valens, and the Big Bopper (Jiles Perry Richardson). Don McLean's 1971 song "American Pie" is about this tragic event.

Q The American game of poker is believed to be descended from what Italian card game?

A At the time of the Renaissance, Italians played a card game called *primero*. In *primero*, each player received four cards, and could bid, stake, or pass. The game changed over the years, and one version was a French card game called *poque*, the name of which was Americanized to *poker*.

It is also claimed that poker was influenced by a similar Persian card game called *as-nas*.

Q What hand in poker is known as a "dead man's hand"?

A On August 2, 1876, Wild Bill Hickok was shot in the back of the head by Jack McCall in a saloon in Deadwood, South Dakota. Hickock died holding a pair of aces and a pair of eights, which became known as a "dead man's hand."

Q What is the highest ranking winning hand in modern-day poker in the U.S.?

A A royal flush: ace, king, queen, jack, and ten of the same suit. In case of a tie, the suits are ranked alphabetically: clubs, diamonds, hearts, and spades. However, a royal flush is a once-in-a-lifetime event, so it is highly improbable that two hands in the same game would be royal flushes.

Q What is the function of the honeycomb of bumps on an alligator's jaw?

A As reported in *Nature* magazine, the bumps that cover an alligator's jaw are sensors so sensitive that they can detect ripples from a single drop of water. Alligators can pinpoint the splashes in the water, and can stay alert to danger, even while snoozing in the sun.

Q What type of insect is kept in apiaries?

A Bees are kept in apiaries, which are places where they build their hives.

Q What is a mink?

A A mink is semiaquatic carnivorous mammal of the weasel family. The mink originated in North America, but is now distributed all over the world. Known for their prized fur, many minks are now farmed. They swim very well, and like to eat small fish, eggs, birds, and small mammals.

Q What is an ermine?

A Ermine is a short-tailed weasel whose fur turns white in the winter. Mice are its main food, but it also eats small mammals and birds. Ermine is also the name for the highly valued winter-white fur of both the ermine and the long-tailed weasel. In the Middle Ages, only royalty wore white fur; the black-tipped tails are the traditional trim on the robes of royalty.

Q What body of water has the distinction of having the world's highest tides?

A The Bay of Fundy, which is an arm of the northern Atlantic Ocean between New Brunswick and Nova Scotia, has the greatest fluctuation in tide levels—as much as 70 feet!

Q Throughout the 1800s, Rocky Mountain locusts periodically ravaged farm fields in the Midwest and Western United States, sometimes in clouds hundreds of miles long. Then, there were no locusts—what happened to them? Why did they disappear?

A They appear to be extinct; the last live Rocky Mountain locust was collected in 1902. Dr. Jeffrey A. Lockwood of the University of Wyoming believes that it was the changes to their habitat: farming the land in the valleys where they lived, the destruction of locust eggs by turning the soil, and the introduction of new plants and animals. Recently, researchers have found intact locust bodies in glaciers, which they will use for further studies.

Q What is a rip tide?

A Rip tides are formed when water that is pushed up on shore cannot easily return, and becomes trapped inside the break near shore. As gravity pulls the water back toward the sea, a river-like current develops, eroding a channel, and creating what is known as a rip current, or rip tide. It is estimated that 80% of the rescues by lifeguards at America's surf beaches are due to people being caught in rip currents.

Q Where is the Bering Sea?

A The Bering Sea is the extreme northern arm of the Pacific Ocean that separates Alaska (U.S.) from Siberia (Russia). The Bering Sea was named for Danish explorer Vitus Jonassen Bering (1681–1741), who discovered the straits while in the service of Russia.

Q Who holds the record for greatest number of years hosting a television talk show?

A It is believed to be Joe Franklin. Beginning in the 1950s, *The Joe Franklin Show* ran on local New York television for more than forty consecutive years! Joe, who also has had a radio show, claims to have interviewed a few hundred thousand guests, including such stars as Bing Crosby, Bill Cosby, and John Lennon, as well as many, many relatively unknown denizens of showbiz.

Q What show lays claim to being the longest-running network television program?

A NBC's *Meet the Press*, now hosted by Tim Russert; it has been on the air continuously since 1947.

Q What show was television's longest running western?

A *Gunsmoke* (1955–1975), starring James Arness as Marshall Matt Dillon.

Q It claims to be the longest running entertainment show in the history of American television. Set in the fictional Midwestern town of Springfield, what television soap opera is the longest running?

A *Guiding Light* debuted on CBS television on June 30, 1952. *Guiding Light* was on radio for fifteen years before its move to the small screen. More than 15,000 episodes have been televised.

Q Where did M&Ms get their name?

A Candy company owners Forrest Mars and Bruce Murrie. Introduced in 1941, M&M's Plain Chocolate Candies became a favorite of American GIs serving in World War II. Why?—because M&Ms melted in their mouths, not in their hands.

Q As of the 2000 census, where is the population center of the United States?

A Continuing a decades-long trend, the center of the population has moved west—to a spot three miles east of Edgar Springs, Missouri. Edgar Springs is roughly 120 miles southwest of St. Louis, just off I-44.

Q How many presidents of the United States were born west of the Mississippi River? Who was the first one to have been born west of the Mississippi?

A As of this writing, seven presidents were born west of the Mississippi River. The first one was the thirty-first president, Herbert Hoover, who was born in West Branch, Iowa. Presidents Truman (Lamar, Missouri), Eisenhower (Denison, Texas), Johnson (near Stonewall, Texas), Nixon (Yorba Linda, California), Ford (Omaha, Nebraska), and Clinton (Hope, Arkansas) were all born west of the Mississippi.

Q Which U.S. state contains the most square miles of inland water?

A With 20,171 square miles of inland water, Alaska contains the most square miles of inland water. There are over three million lakes in Alaska. The largest, Lake Iliamna, is the size of Connecticut.

Q **What are the six states that were named for English kings and queens?**

A Georgia (named for George II), Maryland (for Henrietta Maria, wife of Charles I), North and South Carolina (from *Carolus*, Latin for the same Charles), and Virginia and West Virginia (for Elizabeth I, the Virgin Queen).

Q **When was Kleenex® first introduced?**

A Kleenex Cold Cream Remover tissues came out in 1924, but it was not until 1930 that Kleenex was marketed as a disposable handkerchief. It was in 1930 that Kleenex changed its name to Kleenex® Facial Tissue.

Q **When were Scott® paper towels first sold?**

A In 1907 the Scott Brothers of Philadelphia introduced SANITOWEL paper towels, aimed at the institutional market. In 1931, Scott introduced the first paper towel for use in the kitchen.

Q Which chef/television personality had a cooking show beginning in 1963 called *The French Chef,* and was the author of several best-selling cookbooks?

A Known for her lively TV personality as well as for her cooking skills, Julia Child has written several cookbooks; her first best-seller was *Mastering the Art of French Cooking,* written with Simone Beck and Louisette Bertholle.

Q How did the poet Edna St. Vincent Millay get her middle name?

A Shortly after Charles Buzzell had his life saved by the emergency room medical staff at New York City's St. Vincent Hospital in 1892, his sister honored the hospital by making it part of her new baby daughter's name.

Q Which best-selling author was once a Democratic state legislator from Mississippi?

A John Grisham, who is a lawyer, is the author of many top-selling titles, including *The Firm, A Time to Kill, The Pelican Brief,* and *The Summons.*

Q What Colombian novelist and short-story writer won the Nobel Prize for Literature in 1982?

A Gabriel Garcia Marquez, whose most famous work is *One Hundred Years of Solitude*, won the Nobel Prize for Literature in 1982. His writing has been described as "magic realism."

Q Ferdinand Magellan named the Pacific Ocean, and had the Straits of Magellan named for him. In what year did the Portuguese explorer begin the first circumnavigation of the globe? When did he complete the voyage?

A Sailing for Spain, Magellan began his voyage on September 20, 1519. He was killed in an uprising by locals in the Philippines, and never completed this trip, but his remaining crew returned on September 6, 1522. Basque navigator Juan Sebastian de Elcano took leadership of the crew and led the expedition home.

Q Do any states of the United States have rectangular shapes?

A There are two rectangular states—Colorado and Wyoming.

Q   Where is the Sargasso Sea?

A   It is a region of the Atlantic Ocean, lying roughly between the West Indies and the Azores, from about latitude 20°N to 35°N. It is a relatively still area in the center of a great swirl of ocean currents; it is noted for its abundance of seaweed on the surface and for being the spawning area for both European and American eels.

Q   What former first baseman for the Brooklyn Dodgers went on to star in his own television western?

A   Chuck Connors played major league baseball in 1949 and 1950 before moving to Hollywood. He was the star (Luke McCain) of ABC's popular western series, *The Rifleman*, which debuted in 1958.

Q   When USSR leader Leonid Brezhnev visited the United States in the early 1970s, the White House staff asked him if there were any Americans he would like to meet. What television star did Brezhnev want to meet?

A   Chuck Connors. *The Rifleman* was Breshnev's favorite American show.

Q In 2006, Japanese Prime Minister Junichiro Koizumi visited what popular American pop culture site?

A Graceland. On June 30, 2006, Koizumi, who is a big fan of Elvis Presley, was taken to Graceland in Memphis by President Bush and was given a tour by Priscilla and Lisa Marie Presley. Koizumi even crooned "Love Me Tender" to his tour guides.

Q Do giraffes sleep standing up?

A Sometimes they do, but they also lie down to sleep. It is a misconception that they never lie down.

Q What is a tarantula? What is the tarantella?

A The *lycosa tarantula* is a large hairy spider that eats insects and small vertebrates. Its venom seldom has a serious effect on humans. The tarantella is a folk dance of southern Italy, in 6/8 time.

Q Name the first actress to play M in a Bond film.

A Dame Judi Dench, in *Goldeneye* (1995).

Q **What is the name of the supernatural enemy of the** ***Ghostbusters*** **(1984)?**

A Gozer the Gozerian, a Sumerian god. Gozer has two dog-like minions called Zuul and Vinz Clortho.

Q **Who played "Deep Throat" in the 1976 film** ***All the*** ***President's Men*****? In real life, who was Deep Throat?**

A Hal Holbrook played Deep Throat in the movie. In 2005, Mark Felt, former assistant director of the Federal Bureau of Investigation, revealed himself as Bob Woodward's real-life informant.

Q **How did the Dutch painter Vincent van Gogh die?**

A Van Gogh (1853–1890), who had cut off his left ear in 1889, died by a self-inflicted gunshot wound in 1890.

Q **To which faraway place did French artist Gauguin move?**

A Van Gogh's friend, Paul Eugene Henri Gauguin (1848–1903) went to Tahiti and the Marquesas in 1892.

Q Who played Gauguin in the 1956 movie *Lust for Life*? Who played Vincent van Gogh?

A Anthony Quinn. Kirk Douglas played Van Gogh.

Q What is the date of the New York Armory Show, the show that is generally considered to be the introduction of modern art to the United States?

A The New York Armory Show, officially called The International Exhibition of Modern Art, opened on February 17, 1913.

Q The destruction of what Spanish city in 1937 during the Spanish Civil War inspired a famous painting by Pablo Picasso?

A Guernica. This painting is now displayed in the Reina Sofia Museum in Madrid.

Q Virginia Woolf and her husband Leonard founded a small literary press in England in 1917. What was the name of the press?

A The Hogarth Press.

Q   Match these historic American ballparks with the cities where the parks once existed:

1. Tiger Stadium   a. St Louis
2. Crosley Field   b. Philadelphia
3. Sportsman's Park   c. New York
4. Polo Grounds   d. Detroit
5. Shibe Park   e. Cincinnati

A   1.—d. Tiger Stadium opened in Detroit in 1912 as Novin Field, later becoming Tiger Stadium; it was home to the Tigers for 88 seasons.

2.—e. Crosley Field was the home of the Cincinnati Reds from 1912 to 1970.

3.—a. Sportsman's Park in St. Louis was home to the Cardinals and the Browns for 33 years.

4.—c. The Polo Grounds were home to the New York Giants from 1911 to 1957; the Yankees and the Mets also played there for periods of time over the years.

5.—b. Shibe Park in Philadelphia closed in 1970; it had a thirty-four-foot-high right field wall.

Q   What baseball team was known as the Washington Senators from 1901 to 1960?

A   The Minnesota Twins, who moved to Minnesota from Washington, D.C., in 1961.

Q When was Yankee Stadium first opened? Where did the Yankees play before Yankee Stadium was opened?

A The first game played at Yankee Stadium was on April 18, 1923, against the Boston Red Sox. The New York Yankees played at American League Park (1901–1902), Hilltop Park (1903–1912), and the Polo Grounds (1913–1922) before they moved into "The House that Ruth Built."

Q How old is Smokey Bear?

A In 1944, the U.S. Forest Service, in conjunction with the Advertising Council, authorized a poster by Albert Staehle of Smokey Bear (often called Smokey *the* Bear) as the symbol for fire prevention. Remember: "Only You Can Prevent Forest Fires."

Q Who was invaded in the Bay of Pigs Invasion?

A The Bay of Pigs invasion was an unsuccessful attempt by CIA-trained Cuban exiles to invade Cuba and overthrow Communist Fidel Castro. On April 17, 1961, about 1500 anti-Castro exiles, trained and armed by the United States, landed at the Bahía de Cochinos (Bay of Pigs) on the southern coast of Cuba.

Q On the night of June 16–17, 1972, five men were arrested trying to bug the offices of the Democratic National Committee at the Watergate hotel and office complex. What was the name of the guard who discovered the break-in?

A Frank Wills. The guard had spotted a taped lock on a door. Wills removed the tape, but, when he passed by about 10 minutes later, a new piece had been put on. Wills then called the police.

Q Most mammals have seven vertebrae in their necks. How many do giraffes have?

A Seven, but they are greatly elongated.

Q In the 1941 film *Citizen Kane*, who actually hears Charles Foster Kane utter his famous last word, "Rosebud"?

A Nobody. Kane utters the word when he's alone in his bedroom. The nurse enters his room after he drops the glass snow paperweight.

Q How old was Orson Welles when he co-wrote, directed, and starred in *Citizen Kane* (1941)?

A 25.

Q Napoleon I was born on the island of Corsica in 1769. On what island did he die?

A Napoleon died on the island called St Helena's, in the southern Atlantic, while exiled from France in 1821. Earlier in his life, Napoleon had been exiled on the island of Elba, from which he escaped.

Q In what continents are the following countries: Bahrain, Suriname, Tunisia, Malawi, Latvia?
Africa, Asia, Australia, Europe, North America, South America

A The State of Bahrain is in the Persian Gulf (Asia); the Republic of Suriname is on the northern coast of South America, next to Guyana and above Brazil; the Republic of Tunisia is in northern Africa on the Mediterranean; the Republic of Malawi is in southeastern Africa, bordering Tanzania, Zambia, and Mozambique; the Republic of Latvia was part of the former Soviet Union, in eastern Europe, on the Baltic Sea.

Q What is the name of the world's deepest lake?

A Russia's Lake Baikal, in Siberia, is the world's deepest lake, with a maximum depth of one mile.

Q **The roadrunner is the official bird of which state?**

A The roadrunner is the official bird of the state of New Mexico; New Mexico's state flower is the yucca.

Q **On what island did Christopher Columbus first land on his first voyage in 1492?**

A Although it is disputed, many believe that he first landed on what is called Guanahani or Watling Island, a small island of the Bahamas. He landed on October 12, and named the island San Salvador. He also visited Cuba and Hispaniola on his first voyage.

Q **Where is Christopher Columbus buried?**

A It is a matter of some controversy. Both Spain and the Dominican Republic claim to have the remains of Christopher Columbus. After completing four voyages to the New World, Columbus died in 1506 in Spain, but he wished to be buried in the Americas. In the years since, his body was shipped around to various burial sites, and, because of a possible mix-up, it is not certain exactly which remains are the remains of Columbus. Recent DNA tests indicate that at least some of his remains rest in Seville, Spain.

Q **Where is the only U.S. National Historical Landmark that is mobile?**

A San Francisco. The cable car system is the only one still operating in an American city.

Q **When did the United States first start using American dollars?**

A At the time of the American Revolution, the Spanish "pillar dollar" was the principal coin of commerce in the American colonies. Another widely distributed world currency was the German *thaler*. The dollar was established as the money unit of the United States by the Continental Congress, on July 6, 1785. Only in 1792, did the U. S. Mint begin minting silver dollars.

Q **Who is credited with the invention of the earmuff?**

A Earmuffs were invented in 1873 in Maine by Chester Greenwood. The state of Maine was once known as the "Earmuff Capital of the World."

Q **What is a giraffe's favorite food in the wild?**

A Giraffes like to eat acacia tree leaves. Giraffes are able to cope with the thorns on the tall acacia trees because they have long leathery tongues.

Q Which state's capitol building is a scaled-down replica of the United States National Capitol?

A The Arkansas State Capitol in Little Rock is a scaled-down replica of the National Capitol in Washington. No wonder Bill Clinton ran for President—he already knew the layout.

Q How long did Walter Cronkite do the *CBS Evening News?* How did he end every broadcast?

A Cronkite was on the *CBS Evening News* from 1962 until his retirement in 1981. He was considered "the most trusted man in America" in a 1960s poll. His nightly sign-off was "and that's the way it is."

Q Who hosted *The Tonight Show* on NBC before Johnny Carson?

A When *The Tonight Show* debuted in 1954, Steve Allen was its host. He was followed by Jack Paar in 1957, and Johnny Carson in 1962, who held the spot for nearly thirty years. Jay Leno won the highly contested job in 1992.

Q Who played Mrs. Peel on the British-made ABC show, *The Avengers*?

A Diana Rigg was Mrs. Peel from 1965 to 1967, playing alongside Patrick Macnee as John Steed. When she left the show, Linda Thorson replaced her, but, as competent as she was, it wasn't the same.

Q What town was Jessica Fletcher's home in *Murder, She Wrote*?

A Angela Lansbury, as mystery writer Jessica Fletcher, lived in Cabot Cove, Maine. It seemed like Cabot Cove must have had the highest murder rate in the United States for the years from 1984–1996.

Q What successful film director once played Andy's son Opie on *The Andy Griffith Show* (1960–1968)?

A Ron Howard, director of many films, including *Splash, Backdraft, Apollo 13*, and *The DaVinci Code*, was Andy's son, Opie on the show.

Q What successful film director once played Richie Cunningham on *Happy Days* (1974-1984)?

A Ron Howard was on *Happy Days* from 1974 to 1980.

Q In what Hitchcock movie did Shirley MacLaine make her screen debut in 1955?

A *The Trouble With Harry.*

Q In the 1994 film *Quiz Show*, contestant Herbert Stempel (John Turturro) loses his championship by missing what question?

A The name of the winner of the Best Picture Oscar for 1955. Although he knows the right answer, Stempel "guesses" *On the Waterfront* instead of the correct answer, *Marty.*

Q What city's waterfront is used as the Brooklyn waterfront in *On the Waterfront* (1954)?

A Hoboken, NJ.

Q When was the height of "tulipomania" in the Netherlands?

A The height of "tulipomania" was in 1634–1637; single tulip bulbs were going for 3,000–4,500 guilders—the equivalent of $1,500–$2,500 dollars today. In 1637, the price of tulip bulbs crashed. Many speculators were reduced to poverty overnight.

Q Tulips are native to what area of the world?

A Not Holland. The original homeland of most tulips was central Asia—the valleys of Tien Shan of the central Asian plains and the mountain ranges north of the Himalayas.

Q What is the wettest spot in the United States of America?

A The wettest location in the United States is Mount Waialeale on the Hawaiian island of Kauai. It receives around 480 inches of rain each year.

Q How much rain does Death Valley get in a year?

A In contrast to Mount Waialeale, Death Valley, California, gets an average of one and one-half inches of rain every year.

Q How much money did Americans spend on fast food in 2000?

A According to Eric Schlosser's *Fast Food Nation* (2001), more than $110 billion was spent on fast food in the U.S. In 1970, it was $6 billion.

Q How many carats is pure gold?

A 24K gold is pure gold.

Q How old is Mr. Peanut?

A Planters Nuts introduced Mr. Peanut in 1916. Mr. Peanut made it to the Macy's Thanksgiving Parade in 1997.

Q Who described weeds as "a plant whose virtues have not yet been discovered"?

A Ralph Waldo Emerson (1803–1882).

Q What word is the most common word in the English language?

A "the"

Q Who was Lady Godiva, and why is she famous?

A According to legend, Lady Godiva, an English noblewoman of the eleventh century, obtained a reduction in the heavy taxes levied by her husband on the people of Coventry by consenting to ride naked through the streets on a white horse. Only one person disobeyed the orders not to watch her: "Peeping Tom" peered at her through a window.

Q Match the following familiar quotes to their author:
1. "The best-laid schemes o' mice and men…"
2. "Heaven has no rage, like love to hatred turned nor Hell a fury like a woman scorned."
3. "Oh what a tangled web we weave, when first we practice to deceive."
4. "A penny saved is a penny earned."
5. "Water, water everywhere, nor any drop to drink."
6. "To err is human; to forgive, divine."

a. Sir Walter Scott, Scottish novelist and poet (1771–1832)
b. Benjamin Franklin, American statesman and inventor (1706–1790)
c. William Congreve, English playwright (1670–1729)
d. Alexander Pope, English poet (1688–1784)
e. Samuel Taylor Coleridge, English poet (1772–1834)
f. Robert Burns, Scottish poet (1759–1796).

A 1 – f; 2 – c; 3 – a; 4 – b; 5 – e; 6 – d.

Q Where is the Extraterrestrial Highway?

A The Extraterrestrial Highway, also known as Route 375, is 150 miles north of Las Vegas, near Area 51, where there have been many UFO sightings. The A'Le' Inn Bar and Restaurant is located there.

Q The Amazon River, which is 4,000 miles long, is the largest river drainage system in South America. What is the second-largest river drainage system in South America?

A The Parana River system is over 2,400 miles long, formed by the junction of the Paranaíba and the Rio Grande in Brazil, and continuing through Paraguay and Argentina, joining the Uruguay River in a huge delta at the head of the Río de la Plata.

Q What route was known as the Silk Road?

A The Silk Road, also called the Silk Route, was the name given by scholars to a series of land routes, over 3,750 miles long, that ran from the eastern Mediterranean to East Asia, and was used for trade, and cross-cultural exchange. The Silk Road flourished during from the second century B.C.E. up until the second century A.D., when the trade switched to sea routes.

Q Was Lizzie Borden found guilty of killing her parents in Fall River, Massachusetts in 1892?

A No. Lizzie was found not guilty of murdering her father and step-mother by the jury in the Massachusetts courtroom in 1893 because of insufficient evidence. But, much of the public still considered her to be guilty of the ax murders. In fact, there is a popular rhyme:

Lizzie Borden took an axe
And gave her mother forty whacks.
And when she saw what she had done
She gave her father forty-one.

Q Mt. Everest is the tallest mountain in the world. For whom was it named?

A Sir George Everest was the British superintendent of the survey, and later surveyor general of India, that mapped all of India in the nineteenth century. After his death, Peak XV, which the Tibetans called Chomolungma (Sacred Mother of the Waters), was named in his honor.

Q How many subspecies of giraffes are there?

A Many scientists believe there are eight or nine subspecies, but some scientists think there are only two subspecies of giraffes—the Masai Giraffe and all of the others as one subspecies.

Q How many square feet are there in an acre?

A An acre is 43,560 square feet, 4,840 square yards, or 4046.9 square meters. The acre was originally an English unit of measurement that described the area a yoke of oxen could plow in a day. A square mile is 640 acres.

Q What was the name of the lead character on the 1950s program *The Phil Silvers Show (You'll Never Get Rich)*?

A Phil Silvers was Sgt. Bilko, the con man who ran the motor pool at Fort Baxter.

Q What was an unusual plot device that George Burns employed on the 1950s *The George Burns & Gracie Allen Show*?

A George was often seen in his den, watching TV and commenting on the program we were watching.

Q What was the name of the D.A. who lost every week to Perry Mason?

A Running from September 1957 until May 1966, D.A. Hamilton Burger, played by William Talman, was the prosecutor who lost every week on *Perry Mason*.

Q **What future president hosted television's *Death Valley Days?***

A Ronald Reagan was the host of *Death Valley Days* for a couple of years in the 1960s, but he survived Death Valley, and went on to be Governor of California, and President of the United States.

Q **Who invented the printing press?**

A German printer Johannes Gutenberg (c1400–1468) is usually considered the inventor of the printing press. He invented a system for casting and molding individual letters and symbols of type (movable type) that could be put together in a type tray. Then the tray was used to print a page of text.

Q **When was paper invented?**

A In 105 AD, historical records show that the invention of paper was reported to the Chinese Emperor by Ts'ai Lun, an official of the Imperial Court. Recent archaeological investigations, however, place the actual invention of papermaking some 200 years earlier. Early Chinese paper was made from hemp.

Q Who patented the invention of the ballpoint pen in 1938?

A Hungarian inventor Laszlo Josef Biro, along with his brother George, patented the ballpoint pen. During World War II, the ballpoint pen was very popular with the military because of its toughness, and its ability to write in airplanes at high altitudes.

Q Who invented canned food?

A A French inventor, Nicholas Appert, won the prize offered by Napoleon in 1795 for devising a new way to preserve food. After years of experiments, Appert discovered the basic way to can food. The key to the process is heating the food to a high temperature where the contaminants are destroyed and sealing it in airtight containers (cans). Appert used glass jars, but he had invented the process that was used to preserve food in tins.

Q How did relief pitcher Tug McGraw explain his perspective on pitching to the batter?

A "Ten million years from now, when the Sun burns out and the Earth is just a frozen iceball hurtling through space, nobody's going to care whether or not I got this guy out."— Frank Edwin "Tug" McGraw, Jr. (1944-2004)

Q Baseball Hall of Famer Roberto Clemente died tragically in a plane crash off the coast of Puerto Rico on December 31, 1972. The plane, loaded with supplies, was on a relief mission to earthquake-stricken Nicaragua. During his career, Clemente was a lifetime .317 hitter, National League Most Valuable Player in 1966, World Series MVP in 1971, and he won four National League batting titles. How many hits did Clemente have in his career?

A Roberto Clemente had exactly 3000 hits. His last hit of the 1972 season was the 3,000th of his 18 year career. Clemente was not only a great hitter; he was a great fielder—a twelve-time Golden Glove winner. Clemente was famous for his throwing arm—he could throw out a runner at the plate from deep right field.

Q Al Capone was one of America's most notorious gangsters. On what charges did the Feds finally nab him?

A Tax evasion. Although Capone had previously been picked up on minor charges, the end of his lucrative crime career came when Treasury agent Eliot Ness and his team of agents ("the Untouchables") found evidence that Capone had income from illegal gambling activity and that he had failed to report that income and pay the appropriate taxes. In 1932 Big Al was sentenced to eleven years in prison.

Q Who played Che Guevara in the 1969 movie *Che*? Who played Fidel Castro?

A Omar Sharif. Jack Palance was Castro.

Q Who played Ernesto "Che" Guevara in the film of *The Motorcycle Diaries* (2004)?

A Gael Garcia Bernal.

Q Actor Michael Keaton changed his name, because his original one was already taken. What was his name before he changed it?

A Michael Douglas.

Q Who was the original host of the 1980s music and dance show *Solid Gold*?

A Dionne Warwick.

Q Who narrated *The Wonder Years* (1988–1993)?

A The voice of Kevin in his later years was supplied by Daniel Stern.

Q With some exceptions (such as the designations for the Super Bowls), we use Arabic numerals in the modern world, including the United States. When were Arabic numerals introduced into Europe?

A Leonardo of Pisa introduced Arabic numerals into Europe in 1202 (also known as MCCII).

Q Which United States mountain lays claim to having the world's windiest weather?

A Antarctica is known for its bitter cold and high winds, but New Hampshire's Mount Washington, although not the tallest peak in the eastern United States, probably has the world's windiest weather—gusts were recorded at 231 miles per hour on April 12, 1934. In December 1997 it was reported that Guam had 236-mph winds, but their measuring equipment proved faulty, so Mt. Washington maintains the title.

Mt. Washington's winds average 35.2 miles per hour!

Q Who was the first president of the American Federation of Labor?

A Samuel Gompers (1850–1924), a leader in the cigar makers union, helped found the American Federation of Labor in 1886, and became the first president.

Q How old is the Statue of Liberty?

A U.S. president Grover Cleveland formally dedicated it on October 28, 1886. The Statue of Liberty commemorates the alliance between France and the United States, and was designed by French sculptor Frederic-Auguste Bartholdi. The statue was completed in 1884, then taken apart and shipped to New York City.

Q What is the Walker Cup? What is its connection to the 43rd President of the United States?

A The Walker Cup is a bi-annual match play between male amateur golfers from Great Britain, Ireland, and America. The name of the match comes from the trophy's donator, George Herbert Walker, the maternal great-grandfather of the 43rd President of the United States, George Walker Bush. Walker conceived of the tournament in 1920.

Q What is the name of the "Michelin Man"?

A Bibendum, nicknamed "Bib," has been in Michelin's advertising since 1898, when he was created by the illustrator Marius Rossillon.

Q On what Pacific island were whales' teeth used as money until the late nineteenth century?

A Fiji.

Q Which bird has the largest wingspan?

A The great white pelican, which has a wingspan of 141 inches.

Q What snake is the longest snake?

A The reticulated python is 35 feet long.

Q Why do men button from the right and women button from the left?

A It is a practice dating back to the fifteenth century. Because most people are right-handed, and as men often dressed themselves, buttoning from the right side made sense. The wealthy women who could afford the expensive buttons of the day had dressers, and they found it easier to work from their right, the wearer's left.

Q Based in South Bend, Indiana, Studebaker was known as the only American manufacturer to successfully switch from horse-drawn wagons to gasoline-powered vehicles. When was the last Studebaker car made?

A Studebaker, who introduced an electric car in 1902 and a gasoline-powered auto in 1904, made their last car in their Hamilton, Ontario plant in March 1966.

Q What was the first Hollywood "talkie" (movie with synchronous spoken sound)? When was it released?

A *The Jazz Singer*, starring Al Jolson, released October 6, 1927.

Q Robert Altman's movie *M*A*S*H** (1970) was turned into a very popular TV series. Only one actor reprised his role from the movie in the TV series. Name the actor and the character he played.

A Gary Burghoff played Radar O'Reilly in both.

Q What was the Coen Brothers' first movie?

A *Blood Simple* (1984).

Q **What was the name of the character played by Robert DeNiro in the 1976 film *Taxi Driver*?**

A Travis Bickle, a Vietnam veteran who drives a cab in New York City.

Q **Which nation has won the most World Cups in soccer?**

A Brazil, which won its fifth World Cup Championship in 2002.

Q **Where is the world's largest library?**

A The U.S. Library of Congress, founded in 1800 in Washington, D.C., has over 25 million books.

Q **What is the title of James Michener's first published book?**

A *Tales of the South Pacific* (1947), a book of stories that were made into the hit musical *South Pacific* by Rodgers and Hammerstein in 1949.

Q There are now more than 2000 wineries nationwide. Do any of the fifty states not have a winery?

A All 50 states have wineries. When the Pointe of View Winery in northern North Dakota (five miles northwest of Minot), was granted a license on April 17, 2002, it was the first time that all fifty states have had at least one federally bonded winery.

Q What painting was hung upside down in the Museum of Modern Art for over a month in 1961 before it was pointed out?

A Henri Matisse's *Le Bateau*.

Q When did President Richard Nixon visit the Peoples' Republic of China?

A On February 21, 1972, Nixon stepped down from Air Force One to shake hands with to Premier Chou En-lai.

Q What island is the world's largest volcanic island?

A Sumatra, in Indonesia, is 171,060 square miles and has an active volcano.

Q Which country is the world's greatest producer of gold?

A South Africa, which produces 442 tons of gold annually.

Q Which U.S. state has the longest shoreline?

A Alaska, with 33,904 miles of shoreline. Florida, with 8,426 miles of shoreline is second.

Q What location holds the record for the world's greatest difference between mean temperatures in winter and summer?

A Verhoyansk, Russia, where it is −56 degrees Fahrenheit in winter and 56.5 degrees F in summer—a difference of 115 degrees.

Q What famous American sports star was the one who said, "It's like deja vu all over again"?

A Yogi Berra, upon being fired for the second time by George Steinbrenner as the manager of the New York Yankees.

Q Which country has the world's longest network of roads (both paved and unpaved)?

A The United States, with nearly four million miles of roads. India is second with over two million miles of roads.

Q Who was America's first Postmaster General?

A In 1775, the Continental Congress named Benjamin Franklin the first Postmaster General.

Q In 1913, the highest temperature in the United States' history was recorded at what location?

A Death Valley, California holds the American record of 134 degrees Fahrenheit. The world record for the highest recorded temperature is 136 degrees at Al' Azizyah, Libya in 1922.

Q The United States exploded the first atomic bomb on July 16, 1945. When did the Soviet Union test its first atomic bomb?

A Soviet Union tested an atomic bomb on September 23, 1949.

Q **When did Mao Zedong (Tse-Tung) begin his "Long March" in China?**

A On October 21, 1934, the Red Army (the Chinese Communists) began the "Long March" of six thousand miles from Kiangsi to Yan'an. They reached their destination 368 days later, but one third of the marchers were killed in the battles with the Nationalist forces. This march saved the Communist movement from defeat.

Q **What political leader gave the famous "Iron Curtain" speech in Fulton, Missouri on March 5, 1946?**

A Sir Winston Churchill first used the term "iron curtain" to describe the division between the Communist world controlled by the Soviet Union and the Western world. Churchill gave this speech at Westminster College after receiving an honorary degree.

Q **What is the chemical composition of the Sun?**

A Hydrogen and helium make up over 99 percent of the Sun.

Q What famous pop artist of the 1960s made a guest appearance on the *Love Boat* in 1985?

A Andy Warhol.

Q What was the name of "the love boat"?

A The amorous ship was the *Pacific Princess*.

Q Before Tony Danza appeared on *Who's the Boss?* (1984-1990), what other popular series was he on?

A Tony Danza played Tony Banta on *Taxi* (1978-1983), a sitcom set in a New York City taxi garage. This series also starred Danny DeVito, Judd Hirsch, Marilu Henner, Andy Kaufman, and Carol Kane.

Q Before becoming a movie megastar, Jim Carrey had a part on what TV show?

A *In Living Color* (1990–1994), which starred Keenen Ivory Wayans.

Q **Which bone is the longest bone in the human body?**

A The femur, which is the thighbone, has the longest average length of any bone in the human body—almost 20 inches.

Q **What living creature has the most legs?**

A A millipede has approximately 750 legs.

Q **Which magazine is the longest running magazine in the United States?**

A *Scientific American* was founded in 1845.

Q **In what year was *Playboy* magazine founded? Who was the first centerfold?**

A In November 1953, Hugh Hefner published his first issue of *Playboy*; Marilyn Monroe was the first centerfold model. Hefner did not put a date on the first issue, because he wasn't sure there would be a second issue.

Q When was the first nonstop transatlantic flight made?

A In 1927, Charles A. Lindbergh flew his single engine monoplane, the *Spirit of St. Louis*, to Paris. He covered the 3600 miles in 33 hours and 29 minutes.

Q Who was the oldest astronaut to go into space?

A John H. Glenn, Jr. was 77 when he went into space in October 29–November 7, 1998.

Q In what year did Pan American Airways begin transpacific air service?

A In 1935, Pan Am flew from San Francisco to Manila.

Q Who wrote the Pledge of Allegiance?

A In 1892, Baptist minister and youth magazine editor Frances Bellamy wrote the Pledge of Allegiance (the text of which did not contain "under God" until it was added by a congressional amendment in 1954).

Q 1958 was the first year the recording industry gave out Grammy Awards. What record won the award for Best Rhythm and Blues Performance in 1958?

A "Tequila," by the Champs.

Q Where does Gouda cheese come from?

A The original Gouda cheese is from the city of Gouda in the Netherlands, a city that was chartered in 1272.

Q Where was the world's first roller coaster?

A The first roller coaster was built by La Marcus Thompson at Coney Island in 1884. The world's oldest surviving coaster is *Leap-the-Dips* in Altoona, Pennsylvania, which was built in 1902.

Q Are gorillas carnivorous?

A No, gorillas prefer a vegetarian diet.

Q Where was the potato first cultivated?

A The potato was first cultivated in the Andean region of South America by the Native South American population. Spanish explorers took the tuber back to Spain in the middle of the 16th century, and from there it spread to the rest of Europe.

Q Which mammal has the longest gestation period?

A The African elephant, the world's largest land animal, has a gestation period (time between fertilization and birth) of approximately 650 days.

Q What Academy Award-winning actor studied medicine at the University of California?

A Gregory Peck, who won Best Actor for the 1962 film *To Kill A Mockingbird.*

Q In what year did Walt Disney World in Florida open?

A The ultimate amusement park opened near Orlando, Florida, in 1971.

Q Approximately 7,500 people—mostly refugees fleeing the Red Army push into Germany—were killed in what is considered to be the worst maritime disaster in history. What is the name of the ship that was sunk?

A The German cruise ship *Wilhelm Gustloff* was hit by Soviet torpedoes in the waters near Gdansk on January 30, 1945, in the final winter of World War II. German novelist Gunter Grass puts the sinking of the ship at the center of his novel, *Crab Walk*.

Q At what location did the Union Pacific Railroad meet the Central Pacific for the completion of the transcontinental railroad?

A On May 10, 1869, the two railroads met at Promontory Point, Utah, thus completing the transcontinental railroad across the United States. The Union Pacific had built 1086 miles of track, and the Central Pacific had built 689 miles.

Q When did Walt Disney open Disneyland, his first amusement park?

A Walt Disney's first amusement park opened on July 18, 1955, in Anaheim, California.

Q When did the last castrato die?

A Alesandro Moreachi, the last known castrato, died at the age of 63 on April 21, 1922. He had been a member of the Sistine choir. The practice of castrating boys between the ages of six and eight to preserve the clear tone of voice began in the mid-1500s, but was discontinued in the twentieth century.

Q Why are the hottest days of summer called "the dog days"?

A Named in early times by people in the Mediter-ranean regions, the hottest days occurred near the time of year of the conjunction of Sirius, the dog star, and the Sun.

Q As reported by the Hudson Employment Index in a 2006 U.S. survey, what did employees want most from their employers?

A More money. 42 percent wanted more money, while 20 percent wanted better health care.

Q What player became the first African-American to be a NBA coach in 1966?

A Bill Russell became the player/coach of the Boston Celtics after the 1965–66 season.

Q Who became the first African-American manager in baseball's major leagues, with the Cleveland Indians in 1975?

A Frank Robinson, who was Bill Russell's high school teammate in Oakland, was the first African-American manager in major league history.

Q What city was founded in the third century, had the Roman name "Lutetia," and was the site of the treaty ending the American Revolution signed on September 3, 1783?

A Paris, France.

Q Can you name the major American author who wrote the script for an episode of *McHale's Navy*?

A Joseph Heller, who also wrote *Catch-22*, a twentieth century classic. Somewhat less known is Heller's script work on Ernest Borgnine's nautical 1960s TV comedy *McHale's Navy*, for which he used the pen name "Max Orange." (Heller also helped write the 1967 James Bond spoof *Casino Royale* and the film *Sex and the Single Girl*.)

Q **What incredible new invention could solve the problem of people driving with only one hand while talking on their cell phones?**

A Recently, two British inventors announced that they had invented a "telephone tooth." James Auger and Jimmy Loizeau developed the "audio tooth implant," where a small device is implanted in a person's back molar that includes a wireless, low-frequency receiver and a tiny gadget that passes vibrations directly to the inner ear as clear sounds. The user would also have, outside the body, a small device with a keypad and an on-off button, so the phone could be turned off when the user wanted to sleep or go to the movies.

Q **Which actress/film director first achieved national exposure as the Coppertone baby?**

A Future star Jodie Foster was only three when she first appeared pig-tailed and bare-bottomed in Coppertone suntan lotion commercials.

Q **How far is a light year?**

A A light year is the distance it takes light to travel to travel in one year at a speed of 186,200 miles per second. One light year is about six trillion miles.

Q What is the Kuiper belt?

A The Kuiper belt is a ring of celestial bodies orbiting outside our solar system, beyond the farthest planets, Neptune and Pluto. Scientists believe that the Kuiper belt may be a source of comets.

Q Did Apollo 14 astronaut Alan Shepherd really drive a golf ball on the moon nearly half a mile?

A No. According to duffer's legend, Shepherd drove a ball 1450 yards in the low gravity of the moon. That's about four times longer than Tiger Woods' best shot. The truth is more earthbound: Shepherd's longest drive with a makeshift club went only a few hundred yards. That's not bad for a one-handed shot by a golfer in full astronaut's gear, but it's no world-beater.

Q Which moon of Saturn is the only known moon in the solar system with an atmosphere?

A Titan.

Q When did Mr. Clean® make his first television commercials?

A Mr. Clean products were introduced by Proctor & Gamble in 1956, and Mr. Clean, ahead of his time, completely bald and wearing an earring, was on TV from the beginning. He was listed as "one of the sexiest men alive" by People magazine in 1998.

Q Morris the Cat is the spokesman for what brand of cat food?

A Morris' career began in 1968 when 9Lives® Cat Food discovered him in a Chicago area animal shelter. Morris, who quickly became one of the leading TV personalities of the day, has also appeared in movies, magazines, and books. Morris the Cat has been portrayed by several different cats over the years.

Q How long is the Trans-Siberian Railway?

A The Trans-Siberian Railway runs 5,777 miles from Moscow to Vladivostok and crosses seven time zones. Nearly the entire line is electrified.

Q Which of the following is not one of the five most popular ice cream flavors: Vanilla; Chocolate; Chocolate Chip; Butter Pecan; Strawberry; Neapolitan?

A Chocolate Chip. It ranks sixth on the list. Rounding out the International Ice Cream Association top ten list are French Vanilla; Cookies and Cream; Vanilla Fudge Ripple; and Praline Pecan.

Q In 1858, a Philadelphia resident named H. L. Lipman was granted a patent for one of the most useful inventions in writing history. What was it?

A The eraser-topped lead pencil. Lipman apparently had his eyes set squarely on the future: A few years after his pencil invention, he purchased the copyright for another historical breakthrough, the postcard.

Q In 1868, Wisconsin journalist Christopher Sholes received a patent for a machine he called a "Type-Writer." His invention had one major drawback. What was it?

A Sholes' typewriter was a great innovation, but this all capital contraption lacked a shift key. In 1878, the Remington Model 2 remedied that deficit.

Q **Who was the first philosopher to use a typewriter?**

A Friedrich Nietzsche, who purchased his first typewriter in 1881. The great nihilist's attempts to master these primitive writing machines were very unsuccessful and frustrating. In fact, at least one commentator has suggested a connection between Nietzsche's frustration with typewriting and his insanity a few years later.

Q **In 2002, *TV Guide* magazine put out a list of the 50 Top Shows of All Time. What show did *TV Guide* put at the top of its list of the 50 Best Shows of All Time? What show did *TV Guide* consider the Worst Show of All Time?**

A *Seinfeld* was named as the best show of all time, and *The Jerry Springer Show* was the worst show.

Q **How many quills does a porcupine have? How does a porcupine use its quills?**

A As amazing as it sounds, the porcupine has 30,000 quills. Porcupines do not throw their quills (that's good news), but the quills, which are needle-sharp, will stick when the porcupine brushes against an enemy. Ordinarily, the quills lay flat.

Q How long have cockroaches been on the planet?

A Cockroach fossils have been found that are over 250 million years old! And, it is likely that cockroaches will still be around after human life no longer exists. Cockroaches adapt well to climatic changes, to say the least.

Q Where can you find kangaroo rats?

A There are actually twenty-two species of kangaroo rats, which are small rodents found only in the more arid regions of western North America. They measure nine to fourteen inches in length, survive with very little water, come out only at night, and are named for their ability to leap with their hind legs and tail. Kangaroo rats live in shallow burrows they dig in the sand.

Q How many different species of insects exist on Earth?

A Over one million different species of insects have been identified, more species than all other animals combined. Several thousand new species are discovered each year. There are approximately 100,000 species of insects in North America.

Q Which airport has the longest conveyor belt?

A Denver International Airport in Colorado, USA has the longest airport baggage conveyor system in the world. Its conveyer belt is 9 km (6 miles) long. The airport is also known for its white roof, which is meant to resemble the snow-capped Rocky Mountains.

Q What is the difference between the giraffe and the okapi giraffe, a relative?

A The okapi is considerably smaller than its relative the giraffe, the tallest of all the animals. At just five feet tall, the okapi is practically diminutive compared to the male giraffe, which averages seventeen feet in height. The okapi is found only in the deep jungle, in the rain forest of the northeastern Congo.

Q How did ladybugs get their name?

A Ladybugs are beetles that have been used beneficially, including ridding the grapevines and other crops of harmful pests, such as aphids. In appreciation, they were dedicated to "Our Lady," hence the name. In Britain, the same bugs are called ladybirds. Twenty-seven states have officially designated state insects. The ladybug is the state insect of Iowa, Massachusetts, New Hampshire, New York, and Ohio.